EVERY MAN'S BOOK OF SUPERSTITIONS

EVERYMAN'S BOOK OF SHIPWRECKS

EVERY MAN'S
BOOK OF
SUPERSTITIONS

by

CHRISTINE CHAUNDLER

Illustrations by

MARGARET FRANCIS

PHILOSOPHICAL LIBRARY

NEW YORK

© A. R. Mowbray & Co Ltd 1970

Published, 1970, by Philosophical Library, Inc.,
15 East 40th Street, New York 16, N.Y.

Second impression 1971

SBN 264 64525 1

Printed by offset in Great Britain for Philosophical Library by
Alden & Mowbray Ltd, Oxford

ACKNOWLEDGEMENTS

My thanks are due to the following for their helpful suggestions: Mrs R. C. Allden, Mrs James Comyn, Miss Eileen Robinson, Mrs Hessell Tiltman, Septimus Newman Esq., Collin Rolls Esq.; also to The Librarian and Staff of the County Library, Chichester and the Proprietors of the Blackdown Bookshop, Haslemere, for their assistance in procuring books for me.

Contents

INTRODUCTION

'Somebody got out of bed wrong foot first this morning!',
said the Victorian nursemaid to her fretful charge. 'Now see
you put your socks and shoes on the right one first, or we'll
have you in trouble all day long!'

The belief that it is important which foot is covered first
when dressing is very ancient, and probably dates back to
the days of ancient Rome. It is unlikely, though, that the
nursemaid realised this when she rebuked the wailing child,
nor, incidentally, that she may have occasioned it to adopt
a lifetime's habit. Enquiry shows that most people clothe
the right foot before the left one, probably adding that it
seems to 'come naturally' to do it in that way, not realising
that in all likelihood they were taught to do so in their
childhood, and that they are merely carrying on an ancient
tradition whereby primitive man hoped to propitiate the
beneficent deity whom he believed to have charge over
the right side of his body. To attend to the left side first,
ruled by a malevolent spirit, was asking for trouble.

Scholars tell us that many of the superstitions which to
some extent are still in vogue to-day can be traced back to
the worship of deities in whom men believed even before
they bowed down to the gods of Olympus and Asgard,
Babylon and Assyria. Some of them, it is thought, are relics
of primitive fertility rites, such as those connected with the
reaping of our British harvests. The practices are not really
believed in now, even by those who, to be on the safe
side as it were, still carry them out. But they were of great

importance to the early inhabitants of the earth, as they are yet to native tribes in backward parts of the world. It is easy to see why. Early man found himself helpless in a hostile environment, vulnerable to all kinds of disasters which came to him from he knew not where. Flood and famine, extremes of heat and cold, lightning and thunder, sickness and death, descended upon him without warning. Where did they come from, and why? It seemed to him that he must be surrounded by superhuman beings, possessed of great powers for good or evil, and he must do what he could to conciliate them, to avert the harm they might do to him and persuade them to bring him good. Little by little, he and his fellow tribesmen evolved a system of religious rites and ceremonies which were handed down from generation to generation, changing gradually with the growth of civilisation and the enlightenment of the human mind. To-day, only vestiges of those ancient ceremonies, which once meant so much to our ancestors, survive in this country.

Yet survive they do, in spite of all that modern science and modern thought can do to banish them. Indeed, of recent years there seems to have been a revival here in Britain of some of the superstitious beliefs of the Middle Ages which, it might have been hoped, had quite disappeared. The rites of witchcraft are increasingly practised by some who think, or pretend to think, that they can acquire magical powers through getting in touch with the unseen by means of spells and incantations. One hears of covens of witches meeting on Walpurgis night, on Midsummer's Eve, and Hallowe'en, and rumours of dark, mysterious doings on moors and in lonely places. And the ancient cult of astrology has increased enormously, as can be seen by the fortune-telling columns in many of to-day's magazines and newspapers.

Astrology may or may not be an exact science. Earnest practitioners of the art will tell you that it is, and certainly, when seriously pursued, it involves deep learning and calculation. The serious astrologers pour scorn upon the popular newspaper forecasts. They are, they tell you, based merely upon the time of year in which a man is born, the sign of the zodiac supposed to be prevalent at the moment when he comes into the world. The birth month is only one of the many things to be taken into account for the true casting of a horoscope. Apart from the sun, newspaper predictions take no notice of the positions of the stars, the aspects of the various planets, the ascendants, the 'Houses' in which the heavenly bodies happen to be at the moment of birth, all these factors have to be studied and taken into account, a true astrologer declares, if an accurate delineation of the character and fortunes of any particular man is to be made. Fortunately for the peace of mind of the many people who look anxiously in their papers for news of what may be coming to them, these journalistic astrologers usually prophesy only favourable happenings in their prognostications of 'What the Stars Tell'.

Astrology, of course, is a very ancient philosophy, and many of the superstitions we still cherish also go back far into the past. But there are others which, as far as one can see, must owe their origin to pure coincidence. A man carried out some action which was followed by disaster, or, perhaps, by some happy event. He did the same thing again with the same result. Was it due to what he did, or refrained from doing? He persuaded himself that it was, and thereafter avoided, or performed as the case might be, the thing which he believed had brought the bad or good result about. We can see this kind of superstition originating today, in the 'lucky' objects many people like to carry about, the only difference being that primitive man attributed the magic in his talisman to some occult power, whereas the modern man or woman usually puts it down vaguely to 'luck'.

People who really *believe* in their superstitions must have a rather unhappy time, though not quite such an unhappy one as they must have had in the past, when they imagined themselves to be surrounded by unseen beings all ready to do them evil, when everything they did, every word they uttered, seemed to them to be fraught with momentous consequences. Today, even the most credulous of us only *half*-believe in our pet superstitions. And though perhaps we may feel happier when we don't see the new moon through glass, spill the salt, or break a mirror, we are not, as a rule, terribly depressed when these accidents happen, and probably forget all about them in the course of a few hours.

The Dangers of the Day

THE first thing to be done when we rise in the morning is to get out of bed, and here at once we find ourselves faced with a difficulty. If we want to be amiable and obliging during the day we must get out on the right side. From our earliest years it has been instilled into us that when we are cross and disagreeable we must have got out of bed on the wrong side. But which is the right side, and how are we to avoid leaving by the wrong one if our bed is pushed up against a wall so that we have no choice? Perhaps that is why our early mentors amended the dictum to that used most often today—'You must have got out of bed wrong foot first this morning.'

Having, for good or ill, left one's couch, the next hurdle to be surmounted is washing. If one is taking a bath, singing in it must be avoided until it is over. In fact the purist in superstition would keep one from exercising the vocal chords for much longer.

> Sing before breakfast and you'll cry
> before night,

one was warned in one's childhood—strange how often in those early years the saying seemed to come true! Even if, in lieu of bathing, one merely washed in a basin, singing was still taboo until one had eaten. There was an added danger if someone else should dip their hands into the same water. If they did, a quarrel was sure to ensue before many hours had passed. Our ancestors had a remedy to avert this danger. They made the sign of the cross quickly over the water, an action which, they believed, would make the quarrel slight and unimportant. Still, it was safer to empty the basin and start afresh if more than one pair of hands needed washing. This superstition is one of the few that serve a useful purpose. It makes for cleanliness, even if it does add another peril to the superstitious person's daily round.

Washing over, dressing is the next necessity, and here again the right foot figures in the operation, and the problem arises once more of which is the 'right' foot. A few perverse people insist that their lucky foot is the left one, but the majority of us fall back upon a literal interpretation of right, and the habit of thrusting the right foot first into stocking, shoe, and trouser leg, usually persists through life.

The belief that it is important which foot is clothed first is very old. It probably dates back at least to ancient Roman times. It was strongly held in Britain in the seventeenth century, when it was also thought to be particularly unlucky if a shoe should, inadvertently, be put upon the wrong foot. An accident of some kind to the wearer was sure to happen unless the shoe was immediately taken off, the wearer went quickly out of doors, and some obliging person threw the shoe after him. This throwing of a shoe after anyone setting out on a journey was thought to be a very lucky thing to do, a belief that survives to this day in the throwing of a shoe after a bride and bridegroom or attaching it to their vehicle when they leave for their honeymoon.

There was a time when it was considered to be very unlucky to put on a garment inside out, but this belief has changed in the course of the centuries, and now it is supposed to foretell good fortune if some garment is accidentally put on with the inside facing outwards. It means that the wearer will receive a present in the near future provided that the garment is not turned the right way until the usual time of taking it off. The error must, however, be really accidental —the charm will fail to work if the mistake is made intentionally.

MEAL TIMES

RISING, washing, and dressing accomplished, a meal is usually the next important action of the day. Meal times offer many hazards. Salt, for instance, as everyone knows, must be handled with the greatest care. One must never help anyone else to salt, nor permit anybody else to help one to it. The spilling of it is terribly unlucky, and has been thought to be so for hundreds of years. The Devil, our fathers believed, lurked behind one's chair at table, waiting for an opportunity to do harm, and when salt was spilt it gave him the chance. It was—and still is—necessary for the superstitious to throw some of the salt thus spilt hastily over his left shoulder, when, it was hoped, it might catch his satanic majesty in the eye and cause him such discomfort that he would abandon his evil intention of bringing about a quarrel so serious that it might lead to fighting and death. Legend says that it was not taking this precaution that gave Satan power to enter into the soul of Judas Iscariot at the Last Supper, a legend which Leonardo da Vinci has helped to preserve in his famous picture, where he shows the salt spilt upon the table pointing towards Judas.

Salt, in ancient times, was a precious commodity. It not only flavoured food, it was also one of the best preservatives known, and one can understand why the spilling of it was thought to be so ominous. It is known to have been used in sacrifices by primitive peoples, it was often presented as a gift to kings, it was used in the past to foretell the weather, for it became moist when rain was on the way, and so served as an early kind of barometer. Does not a piece of seaweed, hung on the wall of a house, act as such today? It was natural that primitive man should regard salt as a treasure, should handle it with care, and look upon the spilling of it with dismay. To him it was incorruptible, a symbol of friendship, and when it was spilt it seemed to be an omen that a rift would be made between friends. The superstition has been handed down through the ages, and is still half-believed today.

Salt was not the only thing that had to be treated with

care at meal times. One had to be heedful, when one had done with them, not to cross knives and forks, but to lay them tidily, side by side, upon the plate. This, one was taught, was good manners, and few people stopped to think why it should be so. The custom, it is thought, originated in the days when a man's next-door neighbour at meals was as likely as not to plunge his knife into him if any argument arose. So he laid his knife down upon his platter to show his peaceful intentions, and when, later in history, forks came to be used instead of fingers, they were laid neatly beside the knives, never crossed, for crossed weapons, as everyone knew, were a sign of hostile intent.

The ultra-superstitious have always regarded knives and other cutting implements with respect. Even today, if anyone gives them a gift of a knife or a pair of scissors or the like, they insist upon making some gift back again, a coin for preference. Otherwise, they say, friendship will be cut between them and the giver. Apparently the coin, or whatever it may be, fools the particular devil presiding over cutlery into thinking that the implement has been bought by the recipient, not given to him. And if a knife or pair of scissors be dropped, the person who dropped it must on no account pick it up himself. He—or she—must get someone else to retrieve it and hand it back, otherwise ill luck is sure to come to the dropper.

It is unlucky, too, to find anything of a cutting nature. It denotes misfortune of some kind coming to the finder. The best thing to do in such an event is to ignore the object, cross one's fingers and move on, trying to forget one has seen it. On the other hand, it is quite a good idea to place a knife or some other sharp instrument under the mat at your door. It will deter a witch from entering your dwelling.

Perhaps the best known of meal-time dangers is the belief that it is unlucky to sit down thirteen to table. So widespread is this superstition that most hostesses will go far out of their way to avoid such a catastrophe. Should any invited guest unexpectedly fall out leaving only thirteen for the meal, almost anyone will be dragged in to fill the vacant chair. The old belief is that the first person to rise from the table will die within a year. Slight protection against this fate is supposed by some to be afforded if all the company rise together, nevertheless it is safer to avoid the unlucky number if possible. Usually the host or hostess will try to arrange matters so that neither a person falling out nor an unexpected guest will leave thirteen. It is thought that this superstition may have had its origin in the Gospel story of the Last Supper in the events which followed the Passover meal partaken of by the twelve disciples and their Master. Judas, who rose first from the table, was the first to die as recounted in the New Testament. It is probable, however, that it goes back farther in time than that, for divination by numbers played a large part in ancient religions.

Another table superstition which goes back into the past is that wine must always go round the way of the sun. This idea may possibly have its origin in some rite practised by sun-worshippers. It is a custom still practised today, especially with regard to port wine. What exactly will happen if the bottle is taken round the table withershins, that is, the wrong way of the sun, nobody seems to know. It is vaguely believed that some ill luck will follow—possibly the wine will prove to be corked.

And while on the subject of wine, it should be noted that diners should be very careful not to knock a glass in such a way as to set it tingling. To do so means that someone is drowning somewhere; the only way to save the life in danger is to stop the ringing by quickly touching the glass in question, when rescue will come in time.

OUT OF DOORS

THERE was no safety out of doors for our superstitious ancestors, and some of their fears and hopes still linger on in the things some of us believe and do. Stand for a while and watch the people who will not pass under a ladder reared on the pavement against a wall. If there is a man with a pot of paint or a bucket of water on the top of it it may be simple wisdom to avoid walking under it, but quite often the majority of the passers-by will step off into the gutter, in spite of danger from the traffic, rather than risk the possible ill luck by braving the old tradition. If you *have* to pass under it, you should cross your fingers, superstition says. This may protect you to a certain extent, though it will not avert the fact that, if you are single, you cannot now hope to be married that year.

It was thought to be wise, when out walking, to pick up any bits of metal that might be found lying around in case any witch should see them and use them to work mischief. In the Middle Ages the finder usually carried the pieces home—especially if one of them was a horseshoe, which was considered to be an infallible bringer of good luck. Those who still continue the practice now think it sufficient to pick up the object: hairpin, button, piece of wire, whatever it may be, and throw it over the shoulder, which action apparently is sufficient to foil the evil power that might, otherwise, work harm. There is, however, one important exception to this—the ordinary, everyday pin should never be thrown away, but should be carefully preserved, for

See a pin and let it lie,
Sure to rue it, by-and-by,

says the old rhyme, not so much because one might be in need of the article later, as for fear that it might be found by an enemy who would use it to do one harm, by sticking it into a small wax image that some witch perhaps had provided to bring about one's illness or death. For that, in the days when witchcraft flourished, was believed to be an infallible way of getting rid of an enemy. One paid a witch to make the image, and after muttering the necessary incantations over it, she would hand it over, and one would then stick pins into it in such places as one wished, according to whether it was desired to kill or merely to maim or discomfort. Pins which were found by accident, rather than being bought for the purpose, were considered to be the most effective. Certainly one would rue leaving a pin lying if there were any chance of its being picked up by a foe! It is doubtful, though, if many of those who, remembering the old rhyme, stop to pick up the pins they may find lying about realise what exactly is the bad luck they are diverting.

To meet a chimney sweep while out walking used to be considered very lucky, and in the past a couple about to be married would often arrange for a sweep, complete with bag and brushes, to await them at the churchyard gate after the ceremony was over. This, they were confident, would ensure that they would have a happy married life. How or why the sweep acquired his reputation as a luck-bringer does not seem to be known. It may have something to do with the idea that a dark man should be the first to cross the threshold of a house on New Year's Day, or it may perhaps have some connection with the fact that a well-swept chimney is not likely to catch fire—a chimney on fire was a very real danger in the days of thatched roofs and wooden beams in chimneys.

A superstitious practice which nine out of ten persons still carry out today is that of 'Touching Wood' whenever they have made some boasting or optimistic remark. Indoors or out, if they have said anything that could possibly be construed as boasting they look round hurriedly for some kind of wood to touch. Should they forget to do it, some of those near them will call warningly: 'Touch Wood!' There are those who say that this practice is due to the Cross of Christ having been made of wood, which gives all wooden objects a special aura of holiness. But it appears to go back farther into the past than the days of the New Testament, and it is supposed that the superstition is probably a relic of the prehistoric worship of tree gods. Old legends tell us that the gods of Olympus frequently turned mortals into trees when called upon for assistance—witness the story of Daphne when pursued by Apollo with amorous intent. What more natural then for those who believed in the Olympian deities than to fly to some tree for protection when they feared danger from an unseen power? Whatever the origin may be, however, there can hardly be a superstitious practice more widely in use today.

BY FIRE AND CANDLELIGHT

IN these days of electric lighting and central heating many of the omens that oppressed our forefathers no longer trouble us, though older people may still remember some of them. When darkness came and candles were lit, many direful happenings were foretold from the way in which they burnt. It was deemed very unlucky to have three candles burning in a row, more especially if four had been lighted and one went out, extinguished perhaps by a draught or by some defect in the wick. The death of a near relative or of a dear friend was thought to be imminent. If a candle burnt one-sidedly so that the wax guttered down, forming what was known as a 'winding-sheet' that also meant a death. Should a candle burn with a blue flame, it was believed that some spirit was present, and those in the room would quickly make the sign of the cross to protect themselves should the ghostly, unseen visitor be evil. To look at oneself in a mirror by the light of one candle was unlucky, but all was well if the candles were two.

Sometimes the wick of a candle would bulge out in a curious way known as a 'fungus'. This was an innocuous omen, foretelling the coming of a stranger to the house, though in some parts of the country it was said to mean that a letter or parcel would soon be delivered to somebody in the dwelling.

The fire on the hearth had innumerable superstitions attached to it. A smoky fire meant that a witch must have taken up her residence in the chimney in some invisible form. The best way to deal with her was to place a poker upright against the bars of the grate, if there was a grate with bars. This made a kind of cross which would cause the lady to depart in haste; it was well known that witches could not abide a cross. Cinders which jumped out of the fire were once examined with care by those who were gathered about the hearth, for the different forms they might take when cold had different meanings. If, when the glow had died away, the blackened shape that remained looked like a coffin, then there was dismay and foreboding for it meant that a death in the family was imminent. If, however, it looked to be more oval than rectangular it was said to be a cradle and to presage the coming of a baby. A perfectly round cinder was known as a purse and was hailed with delight as foretelling the coming of money to the person who was nearest when it fell. Oliver Goldsmith, in his book *The Vicar of Wakefield*, relates how the Vicar's daughters were delighted when 'purses bounded from the fire'.

When a fire burnt only on one side of the hearth, it meant to our ancestors that a wedding was in the offing. A fire that crackled foretold frost—many people still say it does today, as they say, also, that one that burns fiercely and roars up the chimney means that a tempest is on its way. A sulky fire indicates rain, while a fall of soot to the superstitious meant in the past not so much that the chimney needed sweeping, as that a tempest which would cause great disaster was on its way.

GOING OUT AT NIGHT

THE coming of darkness, as might be supposed, was a time of dread in the past. Ghosts walked at night, witches were abroad, goblins and other mysterious beings were at hand to bring peril, quite apart from pick-pockets, smugglers, and highwaymen, all bent on causing terror, if not actual harm, to the benighted traveller. There are people who are still frightened of these unseen creatures, though it is unlikely that they arm themselves when they have to go out after dark with the same safeguard chiefly depended upon three

or four hundred years ago—a wafer or a piece of bread
blessed by a priest for use in the Holy Communion service.
Herrick, in his book of verse *Hesperides*, first published in
1648, tells us of this custom:

> If ye fear to be affrighted
>   When ye are (by chance) benighted,
> In your Pocket for a trust,
>   Carrie nothing but a Crust:
> For that holy piece of Bread
>   Charmes the danger, and the dread.

AND SO TO BED

THOUGH the dangers of darkness indoors were not as great
as those that might be encountered outside, there were still
some to be guarded against. Brooms must never be left
lying carelessly about, but put tidily away in a cupboard,
lest a witch should somehow spirit them out of the house
and ride upon them through the night, raising wind and
storm to torment poor mariners in danger on the sea. Lights
and fires should be put out, a necessary precaution still,
though we do not do it today to prevent a hobgoblin being
attracted indoors to warm himself by the fire and break a
few dishes while he was about it. Then, windows securely
shut and doors locked (it was thought wise to make the sign
of the cross upon the keyholes as an added safeguard against
some wizard or witch slipping through them) one could
retire to bed, taking care not to pass anybody if one had to
mount any stairs to get there. For, as can be easily under-
stood, should a person of ill will be encountered upon a
staircase a fatal 'accident' could be the easiest thing in the
world to arrange.

Of course there were still dangers even in sleep, and

various charms were used for protection during the hours of unconsciousness. These varied in different countries, but in Britain they were all much to the same effect, though the words might differ slightly from place to place. They were generally in the form of rhymes which had to be repeated aloud when lying in bed before the eyes were closed:

> Matthew, Mark, Luke, and John,
>   Bless the bed that I lie on.
> If I die before I wake,
>   I pray the Lord my soul to take.

> Four corners to my bed,
>   Four angels round my head,
> One to watch and one to pray,
>   Two to keep the devil away.

Especial Occasions

So much for the superstitious practices of every day. But there are many for use upon especial occasions, quite a number of which can still be met with.

THE NEW YEAR

NEW Year's day, for instance, has many old superstitious customs attached to it. First Footing is known to every one in practically every country in the world. 'The first foot over the threshold decides the luck of the year' is the old saying. Just before midnight on December the thirty-first a person, a man if possible, is put outside the house. As the last stroke of twelve of the clock is heard and the bells ring out to mark the arrival of the New Year, he is readmitted —to bring in the luck. Some people like him to be put out of the front door and to come in through the back, others reverse the process. Some say he should bring in a log of wood or a lump of coal with him, apparently to ensure that the household will not want for fuel during the coming twelve months. Some give him sixpence, to pay him for his trouble, or some small gift, and when all those present in the house stand to drink-in the New Year, it is he who is given the honour of proposing the toast.

There is a divergence of opinion as to whether the 'First Footer' should be dark or fair. Most people say that he should be the darkest male person in the house at the time, but in some places it is said that he should be the fairest, which certainly seems the most logical. However, dark or fair,

tradition everywhere declares that it must be a man who first comes into the house on New Year's day. Should it be a woman who first enters it is deemed to be most unlucky.

TAKING DOWN THE CHRISTMAS DECORATIONS

THE sixth of January, Twelfth Night, had many ancient rites connected with it. But, as far as superstition is concerned, there is only one of any importance still surviving. It is the day on which the decorations put up for Christmas should be taken down. Tradition says that they should remain up until the Twelve Days of Christmas are over if the year is to prove fortunate for the household. If by some oversight it is forgotten to dispose of them on the sixth, they must stay where they are until the second of February, Candlemas. It is imperative, though, that they be removed then, for, for every leaf or twig of greenery overlooked, a breakage of some household article will occur during the year. That could be a serious matter even today, and in the past, when pots and pans and platters were scarce and hard to come by, such a series of breakages as was envisaged would have been catastrophic.

PANCAKE DAY

SHROVE Tuesday once had many superstitious customs attached to it but now only one remains in Britain—a vague idea that it is lucky to eat pancakes on that day. According to the old tradition they had to be eaten before eight o'clock at night, otherwise they were useless as bringers of good fortune. Eight o'clock was the hour of curfew usual in feudal times, when a bell was rung as a signal that all fires and lights should be put out. The fiat about the hour shows how old is the tradition that good luck will come from eating a pancake on Shrove Tuesday.

HOT CROSS BUNS

THERE were numerous superstitions connected with Lent, Palm Sunday, and Holy Week, in the past, but nearly all of these are now forgotten or disregarded. The eating of Hot Cross Buns on Good Friday, however, is still with us. The origin of this is thought to go back a very long way, before Good Friday itself, in fact. The Jewish Feast of the

Passover, commemorating the deliverance of the Israelites from the tyranny of Egypt, coincided with the crucifixion. We are told that Christ kept the feast with his disciples, and there is no doubt that the unleavened bread which figured at the celebration would have been eaten in that 'upper room'. Although Christians postpone their feast day until Easter Sunday—they could not celebrate it on the anniversary of the day on which their Master died—they continued the tradition of the unleavened bread—bread which, during the ages, has developed into our Hot Cross Bun. It is still considered rather unlucky not to eat at least one bun on Good Friday, though those who keep the day as a fast as the Church decrees, will not do so until after six o'clock in the evening when fast time officially ends. But nobody nowadays believes that eating them will protect the house from fire during the rest of the year. Nor do housewives now bake a special loaf of bread on Good Friday, to keep for use as a remedy against several diseases (specifically diarrhoea).

EASTER DAY PRACTICES

WE do, however, still give Easter Eggs to children on Easter Sunday, even if we no longer believe that eating them on that holy day will keep the little ones healthy and well until Easter again comes round. In the past, ordinary hens' eggs were used, boiled hard and dyed red—in memory of the blood of Christ shed upon the Cross—and, if possible, they were eggs which had been laid on March the twenty-fifth, the day of the Annunciation, as these were considered especially potent to ward off sickness. The eggs we give to our children now are mostly rich sugar confections, more likely to cause sickness than to keep it away.

The custom of wearing new clothes, especially when going to church on Easter Sunday, is a very old one, the origin of which it is easy to understand. After the long fast of Lent when mourning garments were worn by the faithful, garments often grimy from having been sprinkled with ashes as well as from lack of changing, people no doubt felt the need of clean new clothes when the time of penance was over and the day of feasting and rejoicing had come. At one time it was thought that ill luck would attend the person who went to church without having on at least one new piece of clothing on Easter Day, and it was believed that the birds of the air, well aware of the importance of the occasion, would show their displeasure at the slattern who neglected the custom by dropping excreta on him as he came away from the service. Later, this belief became confused in the popular mind, and it is now said to be *lucky* to be decorated with bird droppings when garbed in some new article of dress on Easter Sunday. But, in its origin, the superstition worked in exactly the opposite way.

An ancient belief which country people liked to think occasionally came true, even as late as the early days of the twentieth century, was that the sun, when it rose on the morning of Easter Sunday, danced for joy because of the Resurrection, and that anyone up early enough to see it would be especially blessed during the coming year. Sir John Suckling, who lived from 1609 to 1642, mentions this belief in one of his poems:

> Her feet beneath her petticoat
> Like little mice stole in and out
> As if they feared the light:
> But oh, she dances such a way!
> No sun upon an Easter Day
> Is half so fine a sight.

THE FIRST OF MAY

ALTHOUGH May was—and still is by many people—thought to be an unlucky month, the first day of it does not share in its ill fortune. In fact, it can prove particularly fortunate in some respects. A very old tradition says that young girls who crave for a beautiful complexion might obtain it if they go out early into the countryside and wash their faces in dew:

> That young maid who at break of day
> Goes to the fields on the first of May,
> And washes in dew from the hawthorn tree
> Will ever afterwards beautiful be.

And, in the past, those who had won the good will of their neighbours might find a bunch of spring flowers lying on their doorsteps, an offering greeted with delight for such a gift portended good luck. Woe betide the man or woman, though, who found a bouquet of nettles or thorns deposited at the door! That meant bad luck, and was put there to show hatred and dislike.

The rest of the month, after May Day was over, was thought to be very unfortunate for beginning anything new, especially for those who were daring enough to get married in it. This superstition is still held by many people, and fewer marriages are celebrated in May than in any other of the spring and summer months. This taboo goes back at least to ancient Roman times, and some scholars put it back still farther, to the days when primitive men, possessing no mechanical aids to their agriculture, needed every possible pair of hands to plant and sow their crops. May, in the northern hemisphere, was the best month, except in very early seasons, for doing this, and it would have been important that no able-bodied person should be distracted from this supreme duty during the sowing period. And so, the holders of this theory conjecture, marriage would have been strictly forbidden until all the crops were safely in the ground. The tradition, however it arose, has persisted through the ages, and it is still often supposed to be unlucky for weddings to take place in May. As the old folk saying has it

> Marry in May
> You'll rue the day!

MARRIAGE SUPERSTITIONS

BUT if May is an unlucky month for marriages those who heed the superstition have not long to wait: for June, of all the months of the year, is considered to be the most fortunate. In ancient Rome it was *the* month for weddings, and it was, no doubt, the Romans who brought the tradition to Britain. They probably brought, also, many of the superstitions connected with the occasion.

These are legion. It is, for instance, unlucky for the bridegroom to see his bride on the day of the wedding until she comes to him in church—or at the Registrar's Office—and the two are kept strictly apart by their relatives until the prescribed moment. The clothes worn by the bride are important. Whether or not she is dressed in the traditional white robe and bridal veil with its spray of orange-blossom, she should, we are assured, always wear

> Something old,
> Something new,
> Something borrowed,
> And something blue

if she wishes for married happiness. She should carry flowers as a symbol that her future path through life will be flower-strewn, and when the ceremony is over, before going away with her husband she should toss her bouquet among the assembled guests so that the young unmarried ones among them may scramble for it, for superstition says that the person catching it will be the next of the company to be married. Bride and bridegroom together should cut the wedding-cake, at any rate the first slice of it, as a sign that they intend sharing all the good things that come their way evenly between them. Small portions of the cake are saved by the superstitious, for it is well known that if a piece of it is placed under the pillow at night the sleeper will dream of his or her—usually her—future mate.

During the ceremony itself, it is thought to be an unlucky omen if the wedding ring should be dropped, and the loss of it after marriage is even more serious. In either case there is grave danger that the union may break up, through one or both of the couple falling out of love. However, there are remedies. If the ring is dropped in church, the pastor should be the person to pick it up, while, if the loss takes place at some later date, another ring should be procured as soon as possible. If then the husband puts this new ring upon his wife's finger—the fourth finger of the left hand, of course—and repeats again the vow he made on his wedding-day, 'With this ring I thee wed, with my body I thee worship, with all my worldly goods I thee endow', all will be well.

That the ring should be worn on the fourth finger of the left hand is a very ancient custom. John Brand, in his collection entitled *Popular Antiquities*—a work which was re-arranged after his death by Sir Henry Ellis and published in

1813—quotes a passage from a Missal written by William of Wheatley, who lived during the earlier part of the fourteenth century, explaining why this particular finger was chosen:

> It is because from thence there proceeds a particular vein to the heart. This, indeed, is now contradicted by experience; but several eminent authors, as well Gentiles as Christians, as well physicians as divines, were formerly of this opinion, and therefore they thought this finger the properest to bear this pledge of love, that from thence it might be conveyed, as it were, to the heart.

The showering of rice upon the bride and bridegroom when they leave the church is supposed to bring them good luck, signifying that they will never want for food. This is thought to be derived from a primitive custom of providing the newly mated pair with sufficient provisions to start their life together without anxiety. The substitution of paper confetti for the rice rather loses sight of the original purpose of the gesture. The throwing of a shoe after the vehicle which carries bride and groom away for their honeymoon has also lost its original meaning. Now it is vaguely supposed to bring good luck, but in the past the shoe was given to the bridegroom by the bride's father as a symbol that authority over the girl had passed to the husband.

A rather obvious omen of good luck, and one that is very ancient, especially in our usually rain-soaked country, is concerned with the weather on the actual wedding-day.

> Happy is the bride that
> The sun shines on,

is the form the omen generally takes today, but the idea can be found expressed in many different ways back through the centuries. Its origin is obvious, though as a prophecy of married happiness it does not seem to be any more reliable than its converse—that a miserably wet day forecasts misery.

Nor does another old saying, that brides who

Change the name, but not the letter,
Change for the worse, and not the better

deter many lovers from marrying today, whatever it may have done in the past.

GOOSEBERRIES AT WHITSUN

WHY it should ever have been thought lucky to eat gooseberries on Whitsunday it is difficult to tell, especially in view of the 'fate' forecast if one neglects to do so. Not to eat them on this day means that a man will make many foolish decisions during the year ahead, whereas, if he duly conforms to custom, he can be sure of making wise ones. One would have thought, since a goose is often used as synonym for a fool, that the prophecy would have been just the other way round. Perhaps it was so originally, and the first meaning has got lost through the years as in the case of bird droppings when wearing new clothes on Easter Sunday.

WHITSUN ALE

A SPECIAL kind of beer was formerly brewed at Whitsuntide, which our forefathers made a point of drinking during the festival to bring them good luck. To omit the drinking of this beverage would be sure to result in misfortune. When this custom first began does not appear to be known, but it seems to have been in extensive vogue in Britain, at any rate, during the sixteenth and seventeenth centuries. Ben

Jonson mentions it, and old church accounts show that money was often spent to provide 'Whitsun Ale' for the parishioners. The custom died out during the last century.

MIDSUMMER

MOST of the superstitious rites of Midsummer have now disappeared, except among those who are trying to revive the ancient cult of witchcraft—a rather self-conscious occupation in these days, and one which ordinary men and women find difficult to think can really be believed in by its exponents. However, modern 'witches' declare that they are sincere in their faith in their magic power, and apparently they still carry out many of the old ceremonies associated with witches. For them, Midsummer is an important time of the year.

But the rest of us have forgotten most of the bygone doings of Midsummer Eve and Day. Bonfires are still lighted in a few country villages, even though those who light them no longer believe they are driving away the devils and hobgoblins who would otherwise harm their crops. And those who profess a belief in fairies—and there are still a few people in Britain who declare that these mysterious beings exist and that they themselves have actually seen them—do sometimes keep watch on the night of June the twenty-third in the hope of catching a glimpse of them. But there can be few now who hunt for magical fern-seed, sow hemp, set tables with bread and ale at midnight in the hope of drawing thither the spirits of their lovers, or indulge in strange doings at church doors such as are described in ballads and documents of two- or three-hundred years ago.

HARVEST SUPERSTITIONS

SUPERSTITIONS regarding harvest are very ancient, dating back in most cases to the fertility rites practised by primitive man. They are fast dying out in most countries, for modern methods of harvesting hardly lend themselves to their perpetuation. But there are still some farms, even in Britain, that retain a few of the old customs; farms where, when the corn is all cut, the last sheaf to be carted is carried back to the farmhouse and, under the name of the Corn Maiden, or the Corn Baby, is kept religiously until the next year. For to part with it earlier would bring bad luck to the next harvest.

The Harvest Home supper, too, is still sometimes given by the farmer to his labourers, and is thought to ensure good luck for the next season's 'In-gathering'. And there are still some parts of England where it is thought to be very unlucky if the farmer should meet with a priest or an old woman on his way to the fields on the first day of harvest.

THE MICHAELMAS GOOSE

IT is still customary to eat goose at Michaelmas, though it is doubtful if many of those who do so know why it was once considered so important to have this particular dish for the Michaelmas feast. It was simply because, as an old rhyme puts it,

> Whoso eats goose on Michaelmas Day
> Shall never lack money his debts to pay.

A very good reason for making sure that goose should be on the menu on the twenty-ninth of September.

A few other Michaelmas superstitions are to be found in

some parts of the country. One is that so many days as the moon is old on Michaelmas Day, so many floods will there be during the winter. Another declares that blackberries should never be eaten after Michaelmas, because the Devil has then got into them and will make the eater ill. And a rather pleasant idea, held mostly by children, is that when the leaves come fluttering down from the trees in the autumn for every leaf caught before it touches the ground between Michaelmas and Hallowe'en, one will have a perfectly happy day in the next year.

HALLOWE'EN

HALLOWE'EN, the thirty-first of October, the day before All Saints Day, was once a time of innumerable superstitious practices. A few survive in the games children and young people play at Hallowe'en parties on this night. It was a night when witches were thought to have special power to work their evil spells, and most of the doings indulged in by our forebears were performed with the object of circumventing the mischief they might do to poor humans at this magical time. Bonfires were lighted in the fields to keep them from polluting the ground and spoiling next year's crops; amulets were carried by people obliged to be abroad after dark; and nuts and apples were brought into the house, as it was believed that witches and warlocks fought shy of dwellings in which were stored these wholesome fruits of the earth.

The nuts and apples served our ancestors for fortune-telling, as well as being of use in foiling witchcraft. It was believed that if a man or woman stood in front of a looking-glass and ate an apple, the face of the person he or she would marry would be reflected in the mirror. If an apple was peeled carefully without breaking the strip of peel, and the peel was thrown over the shoulder, it would take the form of the initial letter of the name of the future mate. This rite is still played as a game by children, but now it is done at any time of the year, not only on All Hallows Eve, though those who performed it so earnestly in olden times would have told the modern practitioners that it was useless as a mode of divination except on this one mystic night.

Nuts, too, were much used for divination on the night of October the thirty-first. A man and girl in love with each other would each put a nut on the hearth, close to the fire, to see how they burned. If the nuts burned quietly and turned to ashes, still lying side by side, it was a good omen for marriage. The married pair would continue to love one another and live in harmony all their lives through. If, however, the nuts flew apart when the flames touched them, the outlook was unfavourable. The man and woman would quarrel incessantly if they married, and they would be wise to put an end to the affair at once and look for other, more harmonious, mates.

There were many variations of this method of divination by nuts. They all involved burning, and, if old accounts may be believed, they were taken seriously by those who practised them.

Ducking for apples was also once supposed to throw light upon the future of those who took part in it, though probably there was much more hilarity attached to the process than there was in the more serious nut-burning. The apples were floated in a large tub full of water, and those who wished to learn their future fortunes knelt before the tub with their hands behind their backs, and tried to catch an apple with their teeth. The bigger the apple they succeeded in capturing the fairer their fortune would be, while those who could catch no apple at all, not even a miserable little withered one, would inevitably end up in poverty. It is doubtful if this method of fortune-telling was ever taken seriously. For a couple of hundred years, at least, it has been just a merry and rather damp game for young people—though some scholars think that it may have been derived from an ancient Druid rite which took place at this time of the year.

THE WEATHER IN NOVEMBER

AN old distich is still often believed in by country people which purports to throw some light on the winter's weather:

> Ice in November to bear a duck
> The rest of the winter will be but muck

is frequently quoted when an unusually hard frost is experienced in this month. Some countrymen qualify this belief by saying that the hard frost must come before St Martin's Day on November the eleventh:

> Ice before Martinmas enough to bear a duck,
> The rest of the winter is sure to be but muck!

Martinmas itself is proverbially mild, so much so that it is often known as 'St Martin's Little Summer'. There is a legend—believed, indeed, to be a true story—that St Martin once cut his warm cloak in two so that he might give one half of it to a poor beggar whom he found shivering outside Amiens on a cold winter's day. St Martin was greatly loved in his lifetime, and people remembering him affectionately long after his death, said that he must have arranged these few days of warmth at the time of his feast day because he still feels sorry for those who feel the cold.

MINCE PIES AT CHRISTMAS

MOST of the old rites, customs, and modes of divination with which our ancestors employed themselves during the last dark months of the year are now forgotten. But there is one superstition which has not quite disappeared—that is, that for every mince pie eaten between and including Christmas Day and Twelfth Night, one will have a perfectly happy month during the coming year. Only *one* pie a day must be eaten. It is of no avail to cheat by consuming more than one at a time. In fact, it is definitely a disadvantage to do so, for not only will the second pie be useless for bringing happiness, but it will lose for the consumer the happy month the first pie might have brought.

The origin of this superstition, indeed the origin of the mince pie itself, is not known for certain, though it probably goes back to some old Roman custom, transformed to fit in with Christian belief. It is known to have played an important part in the Christmas celebrations of the sixteenth and seventeenth centuries, when it seems to have been of an oblong, coffin or cradle shape instead of the round pastry case it usually is now. Ben Jonson in his *Masque of Christmas*, published in 1616, introduced a character called 'Minced-Pye', which shows that the confection must have been well known in England then, though it was filled with rather different ingredients than those put into the pastry today. Thomas Fletcher, in his *Poems and Translations*, published towards the end of the seventeenth century, tells us of some of the contents of these pies, of which he seems to have greatly disapproved:

> The cloyster'd steaks with salt and pepper lye
> Like nunnes with patches in a monastrie.
> Prophaneness in a conclave? Nay, much more,
> Idolatrie in crust! Babylon's whore
> Rak'd from the grave, and baked by hanches, then
> Serv'd up in *coffins* to unholy men:
> Defil'd with superstition, like the Gentiles
> Of old that worship'd onions, roots, and lentiles!

The 'coffin' shape, it is thought, was meant to indicate the shape of the manger in which, according to tradition, the Infant Christ was laid to rest, and it did at one time contain a good deal of meat, finely minced and mixed with sugar and spices, raisins and orange peel. One wonders whether the superstition of which Fletcher writes was the same as the one still current today?

CHRISTMAS DECORATIONS

CHRISTMAS decorations were as popular in the Middle Ages as they are today, even more so perhaps, for in addition to being a sign of rejoicing, they served a useful purpose— they kept witches and wizards at bay during the festive season. Boughs of holly, the 'Holy' tree, had to be placed in every room of the house, and sprays of mistletoe were eagerly sought after for home decoration, though the priests barred the plant from the churches because of its pagan associations with ancient creeds, more especially with Druidism, though it was also revered by the ancient Greeks. The Church was never able to banish it from the homes of the people, and it is still to be found in them at Christmas time; while unmarried girls still hope to be

42

kissed under it, even though they may not believe, as our ancestresses did, that to be so saluted was an omen that marriage was not far off.

CHILDERMAS

CHILDERMAS, the twenty-eighth of December, Holy Innocents' Day, was once thought to be the most unlucky day of the whole year. As recently as fifty years ago, country people disliked having to do any work upon it, and many would refuse to start any new project on that date, no matter how urgent it might be. Great ill luck was certain to follow for anyone foolhardy enough to ignore the taboo. There is a legend that the coronation of Edward the Fourth had been fixed for the Sunday after Christmas Day, when it was suddenly realised that it would be Childermas, and the ceremony had to be postponed in haste.

We learn from old documents that it was once the custom to whip children on Holy Innocents' Day, in order to impress upon them how much more fortunate they were than the little ones murdered by Herod long ago. This practice disappeared some centuries back, and the tradition of the ill luck pertaining to the day has now almost been forgotten except in one instance—it is still considered terribly unlucky to be married on Childermas Day.

GOING TO A NEW HOUSE

ONE last especial occasion still has many superstitious practices attached to it—that of going to a new house, whether as a visitor or to inhabit it oneself. If going as a visitor, one should take some small present to give to the occupants when one calls upon them for the first time in their new abode. It need not be anything expensive, but, whatever it is, it should be something for the actual *house*— a cloth, duster, an ornament or dish—rather than anything personal to the owner or owners. This gift serves a double purpose. It propitiates the genius presiding over the particular plot of land on which the house is built and makes it favourably disposed towards the occupants, and it saves the giver from the ill luck which might otherwise follow for him should he forget the offering.

This is, of course, a throw-back to the foundation sacrifice which necessitated a victim being buried, often alive, beneath the building being erected. In prehistoric ages, and in the earlier historic times, the victim seems to have been a human being. Later, a dumb creature of some kind was substituted; later still, even today in buildings of importance, a collection of objects, coins, newspapers, or some kind of gadget will be ceremonially interred beneath the foundation stone. It is done today, when it is done at all, with the idea that future generations may find the objects and gather some notion of what life was like for the people who put them there. Few realise how ancient is the custom and what its original purpose was.

If you yourself are going to a new house, not necessarily a newly-built one, and are taking a cat or dog with you, you should butter their paws as soon as they are inside the dwelling. This, people will assure you, is an infallible charm to prevent your pets from wandering away from their new, unfamiliar surroundings to seek their old home. As soon as they have licked their paws clean they will settle down happily in their new abode.

And, of course, as everybody knows, a husband should

44

carry his bride over the threshold when he takes her to her first home after the marriage. Married life will probably be unhappy unless he does so—a folklore memory, possibly, of the old custom of marriage by capture, though, if it is, one would hardly have expected the act to make for married happiness.

A TABOO WHEN VISITING

A VISITOR should never be presumptuous enough to poke the fire or put fresh fuel upon it unless expressly asked to do so by the host or hostess, unless he is a friend of long standing, of at least seven years. Some old people will still look with great disapprobation upon the brash individual who makes too free with their poker or shovel. This, obviously, is some dim, ingrained recollection of the veneration once paid to the lar, the old household god, who demanded ministration from his own votaries where the hearth, the centre of the dwelling, was concerned, and would have deemed it an insult to be served by any careless, undedicated stranger.

Natural Phenomena

IT is not surprising that much superstition should have been concerned with natural phenomena, for primitive man must have found the rising and setting of the sun, moon and stars inexplicable, and the vagaries of the weather, thunder and lightning and torrential rain, terrifying in the extreme. The heavenly bodies were regarded by him as gods, or, at any rate, as being closely connected with Olympic beings, and were the objects of his worship. Even today some of the rites concerned with that ancient worship survive in our folklore.

THE SUN

THE presence or absence of the sun upon special occasions was regarded in the past as a certain omen, foretelling good or ill, and we are still inclined to feel, against our better judgment, that it may do so today. We may no longer believe that a sun god is showing his approval or disapproval of our earthly doings by his appearance or non-appearance, but most of us feel distinctly happier when the sun shines upon our important days. In the past it was considered to be a propitious omen if New Year's Day was bright and sunny. It was also important that the twenty-fifth of January, St Paul's Day, should see the sun shining, for it foretold war and other disasters for the nation if the weather then should be stormy and wet.

A medieval belief which persisted into the early years of the present century was that if the sun shone on Easter

Day, it would also shine upon Whit Sunday. Another, which also persists today, is told in the old rhyme:

A red sky at night
Is the shepherd's delight,
A red sky at morning
Is the shepherd's warning,

that is, if the sun sets, leaving a red sky behind it, it means that the next day will be fine; but if it rises with a red sky, rain will certainly follow before many hours are past, a superstition which seems to have some scientific backing.

That human movements, whenever possible, should go the way of the sun seemed of great importance to our ancestors, a relic probably from some long-forgotten rite of sun worship. People can yet be found who, after an illness,

like to take their first walk out of doors following the sun's course in an east to west direction. If they can make a complete circle, returning from west to east, they are all the more pleased. Cooks, at any rate as late as the early years of this century, liked to stir their soups and puddings sunwise, especially the Christmas puddings. It was definitely unlucky to stir a Christmas pudding anti-sunwise. Only witches and evilly-disposed persons did things withershins on purpose, as part of their satanic spells. Stirring the Christmas pudding, in fact, was a serious ceremony in households before the First World War. All the members living in a house had to assemble in the kitchen where the cook had the pudding ingredients all ready mixed in a big basin. Each in turn had to take the wooden spoon and make at least one stir round the bowl in the right way. It was terribly bad luck to do it in the wrong. There was an opportunity to make a silent wish while one stirred, a wish that was certain to come true as long as one never breathed a word to anyone else of what it was.

The First World War, with its food shortages, put an end to the making of the old-fashioned Christmas puddings in most British families, and most of the traditions and superstitions connected with the operation have probably died out now in these islands.

THE MOON

MORE superstitions about the moon seem to have survived than about any other of the celestial bodies. Will they still survive, one wonders, now that men have really landed upon its surface? At any rate, many of them are still in being today. Nearly all date back to primitive religions, to the time when the moon was the object of speculation and worship, and the rites performed in its honour were treated with great seriousness. Some of them are regarded almost as seriously still.

Seeing the new moon through glass, for instance, is considered an omen of bad luck for the whole of its monthly cycle, and many people are unreasonably worried and depressed if they happen to do so by accident. The idea has an obvious descendancy from the ancient worship of Diana, the pagan goddess of the moon. When the new moon appeared in the night sky, moon worshippers would repair to the nearest shrine dedicated to the goddess, to offer the sacrifices and carry out the rites ordained for the occasion. Those who did not leave their dwellings to take part in the worship would be considered to be very irreligious, and it would be thought that the offended goddess would certainly punish them for their laxity. Down through the ages the uneasy feeling that it was wrong to see the moon when new from within a dwelling has remained with man, and though he has long since forgotten his ancient adoration of the moon goddess and the ceremonies he once performed in her honour, he—or more often she—still feels that some disaster will come upon him if his first sight of the new orb is through glass.

Some people even think it necessary to go outside the house for their first glimpse, a yet more direct indication of the origin of the superstition. These, probably, will refrain from lifting their eyes to the sky until they can be sure of seeing the moon straight ahead of them and clear of any trees that may be growing in the neighbourhood. This, they believe, will bring them good luck for the coming month. Others like, if possible, to see the silver bow over their right shoulder, for then a wish will come true. These last believe that to see it over the left shoulder is unlucky, but in this case the ill luck can be averted by making a humble obeisance, much as the early worshipper no doubt did, when he imagined he had inadvertently offended the goddess.

Turning one's purse while gazing at the new moon for the first time, is also considered to be a desirable thing to do, for the amount of the money one carries will be doubled by the time the next new moon appears.

Many countrymen believe that the moon exerts a strong influence upon the growth of plants and seeds, and they will only plant and sow during the waxing moon except where leguminous plants are concerned. These, peas and runner beans—especially runner beans which twine themselves round the poles put for their support in an anti-clockwise direction—should be sown when the moon is waning, according to folklore. Thomas Tusser, in his *Hundred Good Pointes of Husbandrie*, published in 1557, has a rhyme concerned with this old belief:

> Sow peas and beans in the wane of the moone,
> Who soweth then sooner, he soweth too soone:
> That they with the planet may rest and rise
> and flourish with bearing, plentiful wise.

But peas and beans are an exception. Most things to do with horticulture had to be done in a waxing moon if good results were to be obtained, and there are still a few old countrymen who cling faithfully to the traditional ways. Apples should always be gathered when the moon is waxing, if picked when the moon was on the wane, they would shrivel in the store. Pigs had to be killed, sheep to be sheared, mushrooms were less likely to disagree with the eater, when the moon was increasing. New projects of all kinds were more likely to succeed if begun in the moon's first two quarters. However, it was considered better to cut one's corns, if one had such painful things, during the last quarters. A publication called *The British Apollo*, published in 1710, has some lines of verse about this belief:

> When the moon's in her increase
>   If corns be cut they'll grow Apace;
> But if you always do take care
>   After the full your corns to pare,
> They do insensibly decay
>   And will in time wear quite away.

The effect of the moon upon the weather was thought to be very great by our forefathers, and many of their beliefs may still be found current in rural districts. Country people, especially those engaged in agriculture, look anxiously at the new moon to see whether 'her horns' point slightly up or slightly down. If upwards they believe that the weather during the twenty-eight days cycle will be mainly fine, but if the horns point downwards much wet will follow, for, the rural weather-prophet reasons, the moon cannot then hold back the moisture around her and down it comes as rain.

It is rather unfortunate for those who trust in this prognostication that in some parts of Britain the belief runs in exactly the opposite way. When the horns are uppermost and the new moon lies, as it were, upon her back it means much wet weather to come, for the upturned moon holds water like a basin, and as the orb increases in size the water spills over and descends upon the earth.

When the new moon is seen 'holding the old moon in her arms', that is when a faint outline of the full moon can be descried between the horns of the new moon, rural folklore has it that rain is sure to follow. A halo round the moon at any time also presages rain. If it is close to the orb, wet weather will come quickly, but if it is some distance from it, the rain will not arrive for some time.

The moon was once thought to have an important influence upon love and marriage. Superstitions about these now seem to have vanished, but as late as the last century weddings were often arranged by the peasantry to take place during a waxing moon, a day or two just before the full being the favourite time, for then the couple's married life would be prosperous and happy. An as yet unmarried man or woman could take advantage of a mystic rite on seeing the first new moon of the year. He or she, on first seeing it, could go out of doors and sit astride a gate or stile, and say aloud:

> All hail, new moon, all hail to thee!
> I prithee now reveal to me
> This night who my good spouse shall be?

After which, without speaking to anyone, he or she should go to bed, when, if the moon had heeded the request, a dream of the future husband or wife would be experienced.

But if most of the beliefs connected with these ancient rites have now died out, there is one that is still held by many people—that the symptoms of madness are increased when the moon is full, and that even the sane should not sleep with the full moon shining upon them, lest their minds, too, should be affected. This may not be entirely superstition for some current medical opinion holds that there is a definite connection between the stage of the moon and the state of mind of those who are mentally ill. So in addition to the effect the moon goddess may have upon love and weather, plant growth, and fortune, she cannot perhaps be acquitted of causing madness as well.

THE STARS AND DESTINY

IF any proof were needed that superstition is still prevalent among us, it is only necessary to look at the more popular newspapers and magazines, and examine the columns dedicated to astrology and the telling of fortunes through the stars. It was natural in primitive times that man should have regarded the heavenly bodies with awe and reverence, looking upon them as gods and believing that they exerted an all-important influence upon his fate. The belief attained its zenith among the Babylonians, and from them spread throughout the whole of the known world. Astrologers who studied the movements of the planets among the fixed stars built up an intricate science from their positions by means of which they purported to foretell a man's whole destiny from birth to death. Moreover, they associated the different planets with the various parts of the human body, basing the practice of medicine upon the qualities they attributed to each individual star. In Britain, during the Middle Ages, the astrologer was held in great esteem and almost everyone who could afford his fee had his horoscope cast. Few people in this country now consult professional astrologers, but in some eastern countries, India for example, many place reliance upon the horoscope to decide a propitious day for doing important things. Especially is this so with regard to marriage, not only to select a favourable day on which it should take place, but to make sure, also, that the bride and bridegroom's birth horoscopes harmonise.

But though not many people in Britain go to the trouble

and expense of having their horoscopes cast, an enormous number of them appear to be interested in the 'science', if science it be, judging by the numerous periodicals that run 'What the Stars Foretell' features in their columns. Occasionally, no doubt, these newspaper forecasts prove true—by the law of coincidence they can hardly help doing so at times. But the serious astrologer will maintain that these prognostications are worthless, based as they are merely upon the sign of the Zodiac under which a man is born. For serious astrology is a most intricate affair, depending upon the day and year and moment of birth, as well as the exact spot on the globe upon which birth took place, and the working out of the planetary positions takes hours to accomplish. Whether or not there is 'anything in astrology' when studied with profundity, it is certain that these newspaper forecasts, in spite of an occasional 'hit', need not be taken seriously.

Quite a number of persons, though, read them with avidity, and many women go to some trouble to obtain and wear the precious stones associated by astrologers with the particular sign of the Zodiac under which they were born. According to Alan Leo, a well-known English astrologer at the beginning of this present century, these stones are:

> Aries: a diamond or amethyst
> Taurus: an emerald or a moss-agate
> Gemini: an aquamarine or a beryl
> Cancer: an emerald or a black onyx
> Leo: a diamond or a ruby
> Virgo: a hyacinth or a pink jasper
> Libra: a diamond or an opal
> Scorpio: a topaz or a malachite
> Sagittarius: a turquoise or a carbuncle
> Capricorn: a moonstone or a white onyx
> Aquarius: a sapphire or an opal
> Pisces: a moonstone or a chrysolite

Pearls are not included in this list. Many women refuse to wear them at all. 'Pearls mean tears', is an old saw, and in spite of their loveliness and the fact that many happy people wear them with impunity, the superstitious reject them fearfully. Opals, too, are popularly supposed to be unlucky except, as mentioned above, for those born under Libra (September 22nd to October 22nd) for whom they are definitely lucky. People born under Aquarius (January 20th to February 18th) can wear them with impunity if they so wish, though they will not necessarily bring them anything special in the way of luck.

COMETS

THE appearance of a comet was regarded with alarm by our distant ancestors; rather naturally since the study of the heavens was in its infancy and the unexpected arrival of this strange celestial body seemed to them to be of great import, though whether it foretold good or ill they had no means of knowing. Usually it was thought to be an omen of calamity, the death perhaps of some great ruler, or perhaps an earthquake or the coming of some terrible plague. It is said that when Queen Elizabeth the First lay dying a comet appeared, and her attendants tried to keep the knowledge from her. But she refused to be frightened of the portent when she learnt of it, and insisted upon her window being opened, declaring that her confidence in God was too firmly planted to be 'blasted or affrighted with those beames, which either had a ground in nature whereupon to rise, or at least no warrant out of scripture to portend the mishappes of princes'.

There are people still who believe in this old superstition.

No doubt the appearance of Halley's Comet just before the Battle of Hastings and the death of Harold, helped to keep it alive in Britain. Though if it is true, as is sometimes thought, that this comet was the star that led the Wise Men of the East to seek out the baby born in Bethlehem, it did not always foretell catastrophe.

SHOOTING STARS

IF the arrival of a comet is regarded as ominous of disaster, the sight of a shooting star is generally considered fortunate to the observer. If a wish can be formulated before the star disappears then the wish is sure to come true. In some countries a falling star means the death of some great person, but in others it is supposed to presage the birth of a child who will later rise to eminence in some way. Another superstition about shooting stars is that to see one on the right is lucky, but if it is on the left hand side it means ill luck.

THUNDERSTORMS

THUNDERSTORMS have always been greatly feared by the populace in general—with some reason since they do sometimes bring destruction and even death, though fortunately such times are not very frequent. Many charms were resorted to in the past to protect from thunder and lightning, and even today precautions, relics of old magic, are often taken to guard against them. Country cottages may often be found with the house-leek, a plant of the stonecrop family, growing upon the roof. This was believed to be an infallible protection against lightning, no dwelling with a house-leek on the roof ever being struck. Tradition said, however, that it must be planted with a handful or cow dung beneath it, otherwise it would not root and would quickly wither away.

As an added precaution, when a thunderstorm came at night people were advised to pull their beds away from any wall before getting into them, and then to pull the bed-clothes over their heads, reciting a paternoster while they did so. To do this, it was believed, would save them from being hurt themselves should their dwellings be struck by lightning despite the house-leeks.

The carrying of bay leaves and laurel leaves was once considered potent to protect when out of doors in a thunder-storm, a belief which dates back at least to the days of ancient Rome. The ash tree, too, is supposed never to be struck by lightning, being a holy tree, though some people say that, on the contrary, it is particularly susceptible in a thunder-storm, and one should avoid sheltering under it in conse-quence and should look instead for an oak. A wise man, however, will refrain from standing under *any* tree in such a storm, for it is a fact and not a superstition that most of the casualties caused by lightning are the result of people seeking shelter from rain under trees.

It is popularly supposed that thunder turns milk and beer sour, a belief that is still held in spite of informed sources assuring us that it is the excessive heat which often accom-panies a thunderstorm that does the damage, not the thunder. The old prophylactic to protect the milk was to make the sign of the cross over it. For the beer, a charm in use in some parts of Britain, even in this twentieth century, is to place a bar of cold iron across the top of the barrel in which the beverage is stored. How this is to prevent the souring none of the practitioners of the custom can now explain, but scholars have thought that it probably is a relic of some old Norse religious rite. Thor was the god of thunder in Scandinavian mythology, and iron a metal especially associated with him. He was also greatly addicted to the drinking of mead, so that it seems possible that placing an iron bar on the top of a vessel containing an alcoholic liquid akin to this ancient drink was meant to indicate that the barrel was full of his favourite beverage, and thus induce him to refrain from spoiling it.

The day of the week on which a thunderstorm occurred was noted anxiously by our ancestors. Thunder on Sunday foretold the death of some royal personage. On a Friday, it meant the murder of someone of importance; on a Saturday it heralded the coming of some wide-spread plague. It was dreaded by everybody whenever it came, but if it had to come at all it was better to have it on one of the other days, rather than on one of these three.

THE WIND

IN the days of sailing ships, wind loomed so large in the life of a maritime nation, that it is understandable there should have been so many superstitions regarding it. Many practices were in vogue, either to induce it to blow in a favourable direction, or to calm it when it became tempestuous. Witches were popularly supposed to have great control over it, being able to make it blow favourably or unfavourably at their pleasure. Some of the ways by which they accomplished this were harmless enough, throwing a stone over their shoulder, tossing a handful of sand up into the air, boiling a few hog's bristles, burying sage leaves in the earth, accompanied by various mystical incantations. Others, though, involved horrible cruelty to living creatures—we can be thankful that these, at any rate, seem to have quite died out.

This belief, that witchcraft can control the wind, is very old. There are references to it in the *Odyssey*, where the ability is attributed to the nymph Calypso, who by witchcraft raised the gale which caused Odysseus to be wrecked upon the island of Ogygia. Circe, too, too, could control the wind, and used it to bring the Greek hero to her island.

RAIN

OMENS regarding rain are legion. One, which was once implicitly believed in by farm workers in particular, was that when a cow carried her tail upright it meant that rain was imminent. Another cow superstition believed to foretell rain was when the beast slapped her tail against some tree or fence. The cackling of hens, the loud quacking of ducks, the hissing of geese, the prolonged cawing of rooks and the way in which these birds flew about 'weaving baskets' in the air, all informed the weatherwise country dweller that rain was on the way. Many people still believe in these prognostications, even though the sun is shining in a clear sky and the Meteorological Office declares that an anticyclone is in being and is likely to remain for some days. When a countryman's corns are extra painful, he confidently predicts rain, as he does also when his rheumatism is worse than usual. Possibly though, these last two portents should not be classed as superstition, since changes in the weather do sometimes seem to affect sufferers from these complaints in good truth.

One of the best-known weather prophecies is that whatever the weather may be on St Swithun's Day, July the fifteenth, so it will remain for the ensuing forty days.

> St Swithun's Day, if thou dost rain,
> For forty days it will remain:
> St Swithun's Day, if thou be fair,
> For forty days 'twill rain na mair,

says an old rhyme, one which, with slight variations, has been known in Britain for at least three hundred years. It refers to a legend that Bishop Swithun of Winchester had left directions that he should be buried outside the cathedral church, in a humble position where the feet of worshippers might tread upon his grave as the people went to and from the sacred edifice. His wish was carried out, but when, later, he was canonised, the monks decided to exhume his remains and bury them in a more honourable position within the choir. The work was begun on July the fifteenth, but it rained so heavily that it could not be completed. The rain continued for forty days, so that the monks, feeling that the saint was exhibiting his displeasure at this disregard of his wishes, abandoned the attempt, and instead erected a shrine over the grave. Thereafter, whatever the weather might be on the fifteenth of July, so it would remain for forty days.

This belief has persisted down the centuries and is still not quite forgotten, and in many parts of the country some people still look anxiously to see what the weather will be on the saintly bishop's feast day. The farmer with hay and corn to harvest prays that the day may prove dry and sunny, while the man who depends upon root crops and fruit for his living hopes for rain. Especially for his fruit, for it is well known that St Swithun is 'christening the apples' when it rains on his day, and apples need plenty of rain during their swelling time if they are to do well.

There are not many superstitious practices in Britain to bring rain in time of drought, such as there are in tropical countries. In our climate there is seldom any need to use charms to bring about wet weather. On the rare occasions when rain was badly needed in the past, it was thought that the cutting of bracken and heather might cause it to fall, and as late as in the long, hot summer of 1921, this expedient was resorted to in some of the southern counties of England —without, however, much success. More often we require some charm to send the wet away, and the rhymes sung by children are probably relics of ancient rain-dispersing spells.

> Rain, rain, go away!
> Come again another day,

and:

> Rain, rain, go to Spain!
> Go and never come back again!

Possibly an older invocation still, though it is not often heard now, is one mentioned by Michael Denham in a collection of folklore that he made, published in 1892 after his death, which offers an inducement to try to persuade the rain to stop:

> Rain, rain, go away!
> Come again to-morrow day.
> When I brew and when I bake,
> I will give you a little cake.

A country saying which does often seem to come true is

> Rain before seven,
> Fine before eleven,

61

though should the rain begin a little later, say at eight or nine in the morning, the rural weather prophets do not expect it to stop until the same hour at night. And

> When the rain comes from the east,
> 'Twill last for twenty-four hours at least.

In some parts of Britain an even more pessimistic forecast declares that

> 'Twill last for two whole days at least.

THE RAINBOW

FROM the earliest times, as one might expect from its beauty and conspicuousness in the sky, the rainbow has been regarded with awe and superstition. Usually it is a sign of good fortune, as we know from the Bible story of Noah and the flood, and many people still make a wish when they see one—especially if it is on their right side when they first catch sight of it. If it is on their left it is not so lucky, and it is hardly worth while to go to the trouble of formulating a wish. In Scandinavian mythology a rainbow was the bridge by which the souls of the dead passed from earth to the abode of the gods to receive the judgment their earthly lives had earned for them. It is perhaps from this ancient conception that it was once usual for children to make a little cross on the ground with sticks or stones when they saw a rainbow—the old pagan belief transmuted in some vague way to Christian thinking.

And, of course, every child knows, even today, that if one could but find the end of the rainbow and dig in the ground just where the colours touched, one would find a pot of gold!

Witches and
Supernatural Beings

If to a child of the nineteenth century, life seemed full of inexplicable dangers, it was nothing to the threat it held for our medieval ancestors. Tyrannical overlords, cruel punishments for trivial offences, the devil and hell-fire, highwaymen and robber outlaws, were only some of the terrors that surrounded them. The danger from robbers, unfortunately, is still with us, but most of the others do not trouble us now in Britain, and one terrible fear from which our forefathers suffered has disappeared entirely—the fear of witchcraft.

Witches were an ever present danger in medieval Britain, and people went in constant dread of them. The Devil himself did not inspire more fear. He was, of course, greatly to be apprehended, but after all the Church and her priests were valuable allies against him, and anyway his power was mostly exercised after death and then it only affected wicked people. But witchcraft was another matter. Witches were alive, living possibly in one's own village, and a saintly life afforded no security against them and their evil spells. What the Devil could not do by his own efforts against those who lived good lives, he could effect through his accomplices, the witches, with whom, it was believed, he was in close contact. Helped by him, witches could bring disease and death, plague and famine; disasters of all kinds upon the men and women who were unlucky enough to incur their ill will. Many of the superstitious practices which still persist today stem from the devices our ancestors used to counteract the evil machinations of witches, so dreaded in the past.

THE THREE TYPES OF WITCHES

THERE were three types of witches in medieval belief, Black Witches, White Witches, and Grey Witches—all in some sort to be feared. For though the White Witches were usually beneficent, it was obvious that their powers were supernatural and might be used adversely should they so wish. Also, to religiously minded people, to go to them for help diverted those in trouble from seeking the aid of the Church and the one true God. John Brand, the famous antiquarian of the eighteenth century, quotes the writer of a book published in 1610, a life of the Calvinist William Perkins by Pickering, as saying:

It were a thousand times better for the land if all witches, but especially the *blessing witch*, might suffer death. Men doe commonly hate and spit at the damnifying sorcerer as unworthy to live among them, whereas they flie unto the other in necessitie, they depend upon him as their God, and by this means many are carried away to their finall confusion. Death, therefore, is the just and deserved portion of the *good witch*.

And death was probably the poor creature's fate, even more surely than was that of the Black Witches, whose power to work evil was so feared that they were more likely to be left alone and propitiated by gifts of money and food by those who lived in their neighbourhood.

The Grey Witches, who could sometimes be helpful to their fellow beings and sometimes malicious according to their whim, perhaps came off the best of the three classes. Gifts would be brought to them both by those who hoped for some favour of fortune or healing from them and by those who dreaded their ill will. It is said that many an old man or woman, too infirm to earn a living in any other way, would set up as a wizard or witch solely to attract the sustenance unobtainable otherwise.

PROTECTION AGAINST WITCHCRAFT

BLACK, White or Grey, sorcerers were all looked upon with awe and trepidation. The populace in general used innumerable charms and prophylactics to ward off the 'Evil Eye' which one of the dreaded brood might cast upon them and their possessions. Spitting, for instance, was once believed to be a protection against witchcraft, and up to

E

some fifty or sixty years ago it was not unusual to see some lower-class man or woman spit after passing an old person. This custom depended not so much on a belief in witchcraft, as on a vague idea, handed down by forebears, that meeting with an old individual foretold misfortune and that spitting would in some way protect from ill luck—an idea which was obviously a survival from the ancient fear of witchcraft.

PINS AND BITS OF METAL

ANOTHER practice which persisted until quite recently, and may still be in use in some places, was to pick up any pieces of metal that might be seen lying about, in case a witch should find them and use them in a spell to work mischief. Especially if the metal was in the form of a pin, as we have already noted.*

DEFENDING THE DWELLING-PLACE

IN the endeavour to protect the dwelling-place from witchcraft an elementary precaution was to plant certain trees and shrubs around it. A holly bush, with its ancient association with holiness, was an obvious choice. But holly is a slow-growing shrub and when young is presumably not as effective a guard as when it is full-grown; so it was usual to supplement it by the quicker growing elders, bay trees and laurels. The elder grows the most quickly, but although some people regarded it as a good defence (more especially if the witch was thought to be expert in raising a thunderstorm) others looked upon it with horror as a bringer of

* See p. 19.

bad luck, an old legend saying that it was the tree upon which Judas hanged himself after the betrayal in the Garden. However, as long as none of its wood was brought into the house it was usually tolerated in the garden, often indeed welcomed, for at least it protected the building from being struck by lightning, sent by some malicious sorcerer.

Laurel, too, was a great protection against thunder, and was wholly beneficent in other ways. Bay trees, belonging to the laurel tribe, were the most potent of all. Not everybody cared to plant the bay, however, for it was rather apt to die; if it did then it was considered to be an omen of a death in the house. Better not to know perhaps what was in store! However, those bold enough to plant the bay tree were afforded great protection, not only for the house itself but for those of its inhabitants who had to travel abroad, for a few bay leaves carried in the pocket warded off plague, witches, robbers, and accidents of all kinds. The tree's reputation goes back far into history, and its leaves were used in Grecian games contests to crown the victors.

PROTECTING INFANTS

CHILDREN, it was believed, were especially vulnerable to a witch's machinations, and needed protection from the moment of their birth. Needed it even before they were born, for the mother had to be guarded most carefully lest some witch should cast her evil eye upon her, causing the child to be born dead or deformed. Should a pregnant woman have any special fancy in the way of food, it had at all costs to be obtained for her, not so much for her own good as for the welfare of her embryo child. The old fairytale, versions of which are met with in many lands, of the woman who longed for some fruit when it was ordinarily unobtainable, and who was supplied with it by a witch on condition that the forthcoming babe should be handed over to her to be trained in witchcraft, probably owes its origin in part to this belief. Birthmarks, not so long ago, were thought to be due to the fact that the mother had longed in vain for some food, raspberries or strawberries, perhaps, out of season, during her pregnancy, and her unfulfilled desire had brought about the disfigurement of her child.

Safely born, the baby had to be christened as soon as possible, for baptism was considered a potent safeguard, not only against witches but also against the fairy people, who it seemed were always eager to exchange their own unattractive offspring for an unchristened human child. An infant was safe from this danger once it had been sprinkled in baptism with holy water by the priest, but not even the baptismal ceremony was thought to be sufficiently effective where witchcraft was concerned. Leaves from a rowan tree were often laid about the child's cradle. A knife, or some iron object was sometimes placed at the foot of the bed in the belief that a witch would shrink from harming an infant so shielded. We learn, moreover, from Herrick's *Hesperides*, that a piece of bread from the Communion Table, or a slice which had been especially blessed for the purpose by a priest, would be slipped beneath the cot pillow:

> Bring the holy crust of bread,
> Lay it underneath the head;
> 'Tis a certain charm to keep
> Hags away while children sleep.

We may suppose that the poet wrote with his tongue in

his cheek. But it was obviously a common custom in his day —he lived from 1591 to 1674—and it was in use by country people for many years after.

WITCHES AND THEIR FAMILIARS

SOME animals and birds were supposed to have a specific affinity with witches—black cats in particular. The possession of a black cat must have sent many a poor old woman to the stake in past ages. That such an animal should now have become a symbol of good luck may possibly be due to a vague idea that it may retain some of the magical power witches laid claim to. The reason why the cat is supposed to be the favourite companion of a witch, is thought by some scholars to owe its origin to an old Greek legend, concerning the giant Typhon. Typhon—from whom our word typhoon gets its name—was a fearsome creature, whose fiery breath caused great destruction in the world when, as was his custom, he roared over land and sea, raising fierce hurricanes that destroyed everything in their path. The tyrant's ambition was to gain sovereignty, not only over men, but over the gods as well. So nearly did he succeed in attaining his ambition that, for a time, most of the gods and goddesses hid themselves from him in the forms of animals. Hecate, a mysterious divinity whom the ancients identified with night and who was supposed to associate with ghosts and demons and to be expert at magic, adopted the shape of a cat until Zeus destroyed the giant with a thunderbolt. Thereafter, though she resumed her proper form, she had a special affection for cats. She became the patron saint, so to speak, of witches, as Shakespeare knew when he made his 'dark and midnight hags' appeal to her for help in ruining Macbeth. So it followed naturally that those who practised witchcraft should also cultivate a liking for cats.

Black sheep were, in the past, also supposed to be especially dear to witches—hence, possibly, the bestowal of the term 'Black Sheep' upon the errant son or daughter of the family. This association of a black sheep or lamb with witch-craft is very old, and was at one time very widespread. The Roman poet, Horace, tells of an attempt to call up the spirits of the dead by pouring the blood of a black lamb into a trench at the behest of a magician, and Sir James Fraser found many instances of black sheep and black bulls being used in the necromancy of sorcerers in numerous parts of the world.

Dogs have never been particularly favoured by witches and warlocks (as the male witches were usually called), though sometimes the possession of an all-black dog brought suspicion upon some old person. But witches made use of them in gathering some of the plants needed for their spells. There were certain plants especially prized in spell-making which it was deemed fatal for a human being, even one possessed of magic power, to uproot. So a dog would be brought in to help. The plant wanted would be dug about so as to expose as much of the root as possible without actually dislodging it. Then the dog would be tied to the thickest part of the stem, usually by the tail, and be tempted by a piece of meat held enticingly just beyond the reach of the tether. The dog would make a dash for the tempting morsel and up would come the plant, root and all.

Horses were also associated with witches in past days, though in their case they were but innocent victims of witch-craft. It seems to have been a favourite pastime of witches to ride the horses left out in the fields at night. When a horse was found by its owner n the morning, sweating and exhausted, with its tail and mane tangled into knots, the man knew at once what had happened. Some devilish old witch or warlock had been riding it during the hours of darkness! The only way to stop the practice was to cut off the tail hair, for apparently the rider was only able to mount the steed after plaiting the tail into knots. If the hair was too short for plaiting then the attempt to get a stolen ride would be foiled. Sixty or seventy years ago this belief of the witch night-rider could still be found among old farm labourers.

THE POWER OF THE WARLOCK

MALE witches, or warlocks, were not to be found quite so frequently as were their female counterparts, but they existed and their activities were much the same. Their magical power was supposed to reside in their hair, which they allowed to grow long and would never have cut if they could help it. The origin of this custom can be traced back to ancient Jewish times. The great strength of Samson, the strong man of whom we read in the Old Testament book of Judges, was considered to be due to his long hair, which, he told Delilah, had never been cut from the day of his birth. One wonders if the cult of long beards and flowing locks by the young men of today is due to their ambition to be considered warlocks?

PSYCHIC POWER OF WITCHES

IT is thought by some people that much of the witch's

ability to impress her neighbours was due to some psychic power she might have possessed. There seems to be little doubt that certain persons in the past had the so-called 'Second Sight'—as a few people still appear to have today. It is usually known as extra-sensory perception in psychical research nowadays. Other people think that this claim to be seers was deliberate pretence by the witches themselves. These non-believers say that many old men and women, youth and strength gone, still wanted to impress in order to earn a meagre living by supplying love potions and charms, or by casting some evil spell upon their fellows, their animals or crops, unless they were propitiated by gifts of food or money. Many of these 'Wise Ones' really did have great knowledge of herbs and home-made remedies, and if they occasionally poisoned a few of their patients with their concoctions, they probably cured more than they killed. For faith in the prescription is half the virtue of it, and faith in the power of the witch or warlock, either to kill or cure, was certainly strong enough in the Middle Ages to work miracles of healing or the reverse. As it still is among primitive peoples in some parts of the world.

Nor was this faith confined to the lower classes. King James the First was a fervent believer in witchcraft, and his efforts to stamp it out by hunting down and executing those who were thought to practise it is a matter of history. Terrible cruelties took place during his reign, not only upon professed witches who asked for trouble by boasting about their supernatural power, but also upon quite innocent men and women who, because of some slight deformity, a hare-lip or a birthmark, were denounced as witches by their neighbours and brought before the justices for trial. These justices were often as ignorant and prejudiced as the denouncers, and though there are records of a few enlightened men who refused to find the poor creatures hauled before them guilty, an acquittal seldom did the victim much good. For the people, baulked of their prey, more often than not took the matter into their own hands. The unfortunate old man or woman (usually woman) would be put to 'Trial by Water', that is, be thrown into some pond or river to see if he or she would sink or swim. If the 'accused' floated, then it was deemed to be a sure sign of guilt, and the witch would be pushed under the water with poles until he or she drowned.

If the 'accused' sank at once to the bottom then it was supposed to be a sign of innocence. But as the person probably drowned that way too, the acquittal was not of much use. There are instances on record of the victims managing to struggle to land, whereupon the crowd set upon them and beat them to death—so intense was the fear of the evil they might work through their partnership with the Devil were they permitted to survive.

It seems strange, since the penalties could be so heavy, that so many people set themselves up as possessors of magic power. Many continued to do so through the times of the worst persecutions; and long after witch trials, whether public or private, had died out, witches could still be found in numerous country villages, feared and looked at askance, yet often consulted in sickness, or for the purveyance of a love potion, or some other kind of spell. Down through the centuries the ancient craft has survived, and much of the knowledge of the old charms and incantations is still existent. There has, indeed, been a revival of it in recent years, and one reads in the newspapers of covens of witches who meet by night to practise the prescribed rites which, according to the mystic lore, will enable them to perform supernatural deeds.

Fortunately, in Britain at any rate, modern witchcraft is mostly of the 'White' variety, even though the ceremonies the covens meet to carry out are legacies from the dark and eerie past.

PIXIES, GOBLINS AND OTHER FAIRY FOLK

As well as the ever present perils from demons and witches, our ancestors had another danger to contend with—the malice of goblins, pixies, and other 'Little People', in whose existence they implicitly believed. These beings, however, were not invariably evil. Apart from their desire to exchange their own ill-shapen offspring for the better-favoured infants of human beings, they seldom did great harm to mortals. They were mischievous, it is true. They rode the farmers' horses by night as the witches did, tiring out the animals so that they were unfit for work the next day. They sometimes turned the cream sour and prevented the butter from 'coming', no matter how long it was churned. They were fond of playing tricks upon the farmer's wife and her maids, and occasionally they caused the farmer's trap to upset by scaring his steed when he was returning home late from market. We have the poet William Allingham's word for it that any man so daring as to dig up the thorn bushes that the Little People had planted would 'find their sharpest thorns in his bed at night'. But, on the other hand, they had the reputation of helping those who had won their favour by cleaning up the house or byre during the hours of darkness; and many a bowl of cream would be set at the door of the dairy by some serving-maid in the past, in the hope that, in return, she would find her household tasks done for her when she rose in the morning.

Fairies had a great reputation for cleanliness. They could not bear to see slovenliness in mistress or maid, and a dirty house filled them with disgust. The lazy maid-servant was liable to wake in the night to find her bed-clothes on the floor and black and blue marks on her body where the 'Good People' had pinched her for her sluttish ways. Queen Mab, Queen of the Fairies—Shakespeare calls her Titania in the *Midsummer Night's Dream*—was especially severe to sluts. The poet Herrick, writing in the 1640s, has something to say about Queen Mab:

> If ye will with Mab find grace,
>   Set each platter in his place:
> Rake the Fier up, and get
>   Water in, ere Sun be set.
> Wash your Pailes, and cleanse your Dairies;
>   Sluts are loathsome to the Fairies:
> Sweep your house; Who doth not so,
> Mab will pinch her by the toe.

Herrick may have been writing jocularly, but it is obvious from his verses that the country people around him in Devon were steadfast believers in the reality of the Little People. The belief persists still. There are those who are sure that they have seen fairies, and though nobody now is likely to put out bowls of cream for their delectation, some of the superstitious practices with regard to them are still in vogue. Not so many years ago a certain maid-servant was in the habit, when she had to go across a large field or other open space, of putting a farthing on the ground before she ventured over. When asked the reason for this curious action, she said it was so that she would not be 'Pixy-led'.

The farthing apparently was not so much intended as a bribe, as of a guarantee of good faith, for it was always picked up again on the return journey. The correspondent who contributes this anecdote concludes: 'I imagine that she did not use the farthing as a coin, but as a handy piece of metal which had the property of averting the fairy influence.'

To be pixy-led was an ever present danger to our forebears, and of all the fairy beings who delighted in this form of mischief, Puck, or Robin Goodfellow, was the most to be feared. His favourite amusement seems to have been to lead people astray. With his will-o'-the-wisp lantern he would entice them into thickets of thorn and bramble, usually leaving them at the end stuck fast in boggy mud, to extricate themselves and find their way home as best they might. If a farthing could preserve the traveller from such an unpleasant experience it was money well spent—more especially if, as in the case of the maid-servant mentioned above, the coin could be retrieved when the journey was safely accomplished.

We can find many traces of this one-time wide-spread belief in these fairy beings in the folk-lore names of our countryside. We have fairy bedstraw, foxgloves (folk gloves), green-man orchid, and ragged robin (after Robin Goodfellow) among our wild flowers. The dark rings in pasture meadows, which we know now are caused by mushrooms and toadstools, are still often called fairy-rings, from our ancestors' belief that they were made by the fairy people dancing in a circle on moonlit nights. When a ring of this kind was found with toadstools growing in a perfect circle, it was thought to be a grand opportunity to make a wish. The wisher stood in the centre of the ring, and with tight-shut eyes formulated a silent wish. If he had a companion with him to say 'Wishes come true!' while his eyes were still shut, the wish was bound to be fulfilled.

Children play this game to this day, as they do also with regard to wishing-wells, which were supposed to be guarded by fairies who, in return for some small coin dropped into the water, would attend to the granting of the wish. Mortals, in these days, seem to have grown more thrifty than they were in our ancestors' time, for it is usually only a pin that the child throws into the well when making a wish. Wishes in the toadstool ring, however, are quite free. In either case, whether the wish is made by the well or in the ring, the wisher must never say what was wished for until it has come about.

If pixies, elves, and fairies were usually harmless, goblins were a very different kind of sprite. They were hideously ugly to begin with, and full of malice and ill will to human beings. They were supposed to live mostly underground, in mines or mountain caves, where they hoarded stolen treasure, sallying forth from time to time to frighten belated wanderers, or to work great harm to mortals who had, by some fault of omission or commission, given them power to do so. Such power could be given, it was thought, if Christmas decorations were left up after Candlemas Day, February the second. If even so much as one leaf should be left lying in some corner of a house, a malicious goblin would have the power to enter through the keyhole and do all kinds of wicked things—set the chimney on fire, spill the milk, crack the wine bottles, smash the china, and even let loose rats and mice in the larder to eat up all the food. It was no wonder that people resorted to spells and charms to keep goblins at bay.

It is from Herrick again that we learn what some of these charms were. Having cleared away every trace of the holly, ivy, rosemary and mistletoe, the careful housewife then brought in branches of box to take their place. These had to be followed by yew, then by birch leaves, and flowers in their seasons, until it was time to think of Christmas holly again. To keep the house thus decorated was helpful in keeping away the malicious little creatures, but there was a more potent charm still. The Yule log was never allowed quite to burn to ash, but a part kept to kindle the fire for Christmas the next year. This, carefully preserved, was not only a powerful safeguard against goblins, but, Herrick tells us,

> Where 'tis safely kept, the Fiend
> Can do no mischiefe there.

Yet another helpful rite that the inhabitants of a house were advised by Herrick to perform he describes in one of his *Hesperides* verses:

> In the morning when ye rise,
> Wash your hands and cleanse your eyes.
> Next be sure ye have a care
> To disperse the water farre,
> For as farre as that doth light,
> So farre keepes the evill Spright.

Trades and Professions

PRACTICALLY every trade and profession under the sun had its superstitions in the past, and traces of them can still be seen in the procedures followed by their practitioners today.

Even the lawyer, hard-headed and matter of fact though he usually is, has at least one or two of them. Long ago, when a deed was being completed, the assignor was required to hand over to the assignee, or his representative, a piece of wood or a sod of earth as a symbol of the land being conveyed. Nowadays, the wood and earth are dispensed with, but the lawyer still requires that the assignor shall place his thumb upon a seal affixed to the document, saying aloud: 'I deliver this as my act and deed.' And when witnesses are required of the signing of a will or other important document, they are instructed to fix their eyes upon the actual signing, in order that they may testify afterwards, should it be necessary, that they saw the action done with their own eyes. It is not sufficient that they were present in the room when the signature was made. They must be able to swear upon oath that they actually saw it written.

THE SEA

OF all the occupations man is concerned with, that connected with the sea has perhaps the most superstitions attached to it. In the past, every old seaman worth his salt believed in the sea serpent, and even today there are some who still believe in it. Even today a baby's caul, the membrane covering the heads of some infants at birth, can still fetch a price, for tradition declares that the fortunate owner of such an object will never be drowned. And there is still an uneasy feeling among both seamen and passengers when a voyage begins on a Friday. If the Friday happens also to be the thirteenth day of the month, apprehension is doubly strong.

Whistling is a thing no seaman likes to indulge in when at sea; if any forgetful person does so, he will be sharply rebuked, for he is inviting the storm fiends to molest the vessel. There is, however, one exception to this taboo. In the event of a sailing ship being becalmed it is quite in order for her crew to 'whistle for the wind' to arise and fill the sails. Care has to be taken, though, not to overdo the whistling, but to stop as soon as the vessel is on her way again. It is probable that the inn sign, The Pig And Whistle, owes its origin to this superstition—a gesture of bravado, as though now the sailor is safe on land the ill luck brought about by whistling is no longer a menace. The sign, in fact, was a double gesture of defiance, for sailors never liked to call a pig, a pig. It was thought to be unlucky to do so, and the animals were always referred to as hogs or sows.

To have a corpse on board was once thought to be very unlucky, and crews have been known to mutiny in the past when the vessel was required to carry a dead person. Legend has it that the late owner of the body feared that it was not going to receive Christian burial if it was not ceremoniously disposed of within a few days of the spirit leaving it, and he or she took steps to wreck the ship to ensure that the corpse was no longer above the surface. In this way the disembodied spirit could at least make sure that its late habitation would not become the dwelling-place of some devil who might hinder his regaining possession of it at the Judgment Day. Although this medieval reasoning is now a thing of the past, many sailors still feel a vague uneasiness at having a corpse aboard.

Many birds and marine creatures were thought to be lucky or unlucky by those who sailed the seas—perhaps some of them still are. Porpoises were regarded as infallible weather prophets by mariners in the past. If a school of them was seen playing around a ship in fine weather, it was viewed with alarm, for it was thought that they presaged the advent of a terrible storm. On the other hand, if the creatures appeared when a storm was already raging, they brought comfort and reassurance to the storm-tossed crew, for their presence meant that fair weather was approaching. Thomas Pennant, writing during the eighteenth century, mentions this belief in his *British Zoology*, and there is a reference to it a century earlier in a play by Edward Ravenscroft. It seems to have been regarded as an established fact in his time that it was possible to foretell the weather from the behaviour of porpoises.

Birds brought luck or ill luck to the seaman according to their species. The petrel was definitely an unlucky bird for him. It was supposed always to presage a storm; so certain was the case for this established that the bird gained the epithet of 'Stormy Petrel', a name which is still applied to it today. On the other hand, the albatross is commonly a bird of good luck, bringing fair weather and favouring winds to the ship that encounters it on its voyage. But it is terribly unlucky to kill it, as we know from Coleridge's poem, *The Ancient Mariner*, which gives a graphic account of the superstition attached to such an ill deed.

The kingfisher is wholly fortunate, whether it is met with on river or around the coast. It is sometimes known as the halcyon, a word derived from the Greek language. An ancient legend said that it built a floating nest on the sea, and that the ocean, out of consideration for the mother bird, remained calm during the hatching period. We still talk of the 'halcyon days', meaning a time of peace and calm and happiness—an example of how traces of a superstition linger on, long after belief in it has vanished.

Fishermen, especially deep sea fishermen, share in all the sailors' superstitious notions, and add others of their own. They dislike meeting a woman on their way to their boats in the early morning, especially a strange woman. It means, apparently, that they will catch no fish on the voyage, or if they do that the catch will be small. Stones with holes in them are sometimes found on the sea shore, and these are greatly prized by fishermen. They are considered to be luck-bringers, and are often carried in fishing-boats to ensure good fortune for the crews, bringing them safely home and giving them good catches.

The man who fishes with rod and line, whether in fresh or salt water, shares in many of the deep sea fisherman's beliefs in the things that may or may not bring him good fortune. If he is of a superstitious nature he will not count the fish he catches until the day's fishing is over. If he does so earlier his luck will change and he will not get another bite that day, no matter how well the fish are rising for other anglers.

Superstitions about sailors are not confined to the men themselves. Landsmen and landswomen once thought it very unlucky to meet a sailor in uniform away from the sea. If they were so unfortunate as to do so the only way to avoid ill luck was to spit on the ground and pinch him. Even as late as the present century this custom still persisted. Not the spitting—that happily is taboo now except among a very small part of the population. But there are people who remember being instructed in their childhood by their nursemaids that it was necessary to pinch a sailor if they happened to meet one in their walks abroad.

One wonders what could have been the origin of such a curious custom. One suggestion which seems feasible is that it may date back to the days when voyages lasted for many years, during which time no news could reach the relatives on land to say whether the sailor was alive or dead.

Many a man must have been given up as dead who, after a long lapse of time, reappeared on his family's doorstep. The first reaction might have been that it was a ghost his relatives were seeing, and to calm their fears the sailor may well have invited them to pinch him to see if he were not alive. Do we not still at times, when startled by some sudden news of good fortune, exclaim: 'Pinch me and let me see if I am awake or dreaming!'? It seems possible that this particular superstition may have arisen in some such way.

THE THEATRE

NEXT to the sea, the theatrical profession appears to be the most prolific in superstitious practices. As at sea, whistling in the theatre is looked upon with horror. No play is likely to succeed if the actors whistle during rehearsals, or in their dressing-rooms while the play is in progress. Real flowers, real food, real drink, real jewellery is shunned by the superstitious players, imitations of all these things must be used instead. The last line of any play must never be spoken until the dress rehearsal. Until quite recently, the professional actor or actress avoided ever quoting anything from the play of *Macbeth*, and disliked taking part in it. It was regarded as an unlucky play. That superstition, however, seems to have disappeared of late, possibly due to the fact that there have been some notable performances of this tragedy.

Theatrical people dislike plays that have the word 'thirteen' in the title, and some say that the word 'peacock' is very unlucky. But, of course, these two words have unlucky connotations for many persons who have no connection with the theatre, so perhaps they cannot be counted as belonging particularly to the theatrical profession. One superstition, though, is quite confined to it—that is that it brings extraordinary success in acting to anyone who sees the Drury Lane Ghost.

And, of course, no one should open an umbrella in the theatre unless it is required in the action of the play. If it is raining when one leaves, one must step over the threshold, even if there is no porch to give shelter, before venturing to put it up.

DOMESTIC SUPERSTITIONS

COOKS, housewives, washer-women, all have their special charms, spells, and taboos. Superstition decrees that cooks should always stir in the same way as the sun's rotation. Should they stir withershins, whether by accident or intent, the cake mixture will not rise properly, the pudding will be spoilt, the soup burnt or otherwise made uneatable. If eggs are used the shells should always be burnt or buried. If put into the dustbin or thrown on a rubbish heap, a witch may come along and retrieve them to use for some evil purpose. To allow milk to boil over is very unlucky—it certainly is, since, in addition to the loss of the milk, saucepan and stove will need extra cleaning. It does not, however, necessarily mean a death in the house, as the superstitious once believed. Nobody can expect to bake a good cake on a Sunday, and if when one is washing up the dishes one is unlucky enough to break something, and it is the second break in the day, one had better hunt at once for some old cracked piece of crockery or an empty jam jar and smash it deliberately. For, as everyone knows, two broken articles mean that a third break will doubtless follow, so it is better to make sure that it is something of little value, and not a piece of the best glass or china.

When sweeping a room, housewives should always sweep towards the fireplace, never towards the door. It is bad luck to reverse this process. When making beds, mattresses should never be turned on a Friday or a Sunday. Sunday is taboo, of course, because of the biblical prohibition of working on the Sabbath—the Jewish Sabbath being transferred to the first day of the week in Christian practice— and Friday because of the general bad luck attributed to it. Many people consider that this attribute of Friday is due to its being the day of the Crucifixion, but the belief in its ill luck probably goes much farther back in history, and may have something to do with the sacrifices offered to the goddess Friga in Norse mythology.

The breaking of a mirror means seven years of bad luck unless something is done to avert the evil. There is, however, a remedy if one is fortunate enough to live anywhere near a river or fast-running stream. If every bit of the broken glass is gathered up and thrown into the water, the current will carry the ill fortune harmlessly away.

Washer-women like, if possible, to wash their clothes and other articles on a Monday. There is an old rhyme extant about this preference:

> They that wash on Monday
>   Have all the week to dry;
> They that wash on Tuesday
>   Are not so much awry;
> They that wash on Wednesday
>   Are like to wash for woe;
> They that wash on Thursday
>   Have little time to go;
> They that wash on Friday
>   Must wash in haste and speed;
> They that wash on Saturday,
>   Oh, they are sluts indeed!

There does not seem to be a couplet referring to washing on a Sunday. But that is hardly surprising. In the past even the most slatternly woman would not have dared to do her weekly wash on such a holy day.

In the years before soap flakes and soap powders were in common use, it was thought to be unlucky to let the cake of soap slip out of the hands when washing linen. If a careless washer let it slip once she might expect some small misfortune. If twice a mishap somewhat more ominous. But if in the course of one washing session the soap eluded her grasp three times, great alarm would be felt by the superstitious, for it foreshadowed some great disaster shortly to occur.

A TRADER'S SUPERSTITION

A COMMON custom among pedlars, barrow-boys, and other dealers, is to spit upon the first money they take when they begin their day's business. This, they think, will bring them good luck, more especially if they put the first coin aside and do not give it in change during the day. Once it was customary for two people when striking a bargain to spit on the ground and then shake hands by way of sealing it. The shaking of hands after agreement is still often seen, though the spitting is now usually dispensed with. Belief in the efficacy of spitting as a bringer of good luck, or of averting ill, goes far back in human history. References to it are found in the writings of many old Roman authors, where it usually denoted a wish to bring good fortune to the person spat upon. Later it became an act of defiance, as it is today on the rare occasions when it occurs away from the dealers in the markets. The act of spitting is a good example of a change in superstitious beliefs and, incidentally, of the futility of superstitious customs. Once it was thought to bring good luck to those who were treated to it, to protect from witchcraft, to show welcome to visitors. Now it signifies contempt and aversion. Only in the matter of 'first money' is its original status as a fortune bringer still maintained.

PROTECTING CHILDREN

ALTHOUGH small children are perhaps the only human beings who are entirely free from superstition—at least until they acquire it from their elders—superstitions themselves have gathered thick about them. They are no longer passed naked through split trees to cure hernias and rickets or held over fires to keep them safe from evil spirits and to save them from fatal accidents by fire in later life. The coral necklaces which some of them still wear are given for ornament only, not to protect them from witchcraft as in the past. But it is not uncommon for mothers still to insist that an infant shall be carried *upstairs* before it is taken down to ensure that the child will rise in life, not descend. (Should no convenient stair be available, it is thought to be sufficient that the person holding the child shall stand upon a chair, or mount a few rungs of a ladder.) A first baby is watched anxiously to see how many teeth are cut before the first birthday; for the number of teeth that are through by then indicate the number of brothers and sisters to come. And it is still half-believed by some people that the child who does not cry when christened will grow up naughty and disobedient, since the holy water has failed to exorcise the evil spirit with which all of us are supposed to be born! The louder an infant wails at the baptismal service, the more certain it is that the Devil has been expelled.

Some Animal Superstitions

ANIMALS of all kinds have played such a large part in the world's story that it is not surprising that man—the most advanced animal of all—should have woven a vast amount of superstitious ideas around them. Of the animals to be found in the British Isles, whether wild or domesticated, there can be hardly a species to which some superstition is not attached.

THE HORSE

FIRST in importance, as far as domesticated animals are concerned, is the horse. Without the assistance of horses in transport and cultivation man's progress might have been greatly retarded. The horse has always been prized above all the other creatures that man has tamed. It was at one time an object of worship to the ancient Greeks, who regarded it as a symbol of their goddess Artemis, and many of the superstitions attached to it in later days probably owe their origin to early religious rites.

It is not known exactly when the practice of putting iron shoes on horses to protect their hooves first began, but it is of very ancient origin, and there is some evidence that Celtic tribes used it in Britain before the Romans came to these shores. Nor is it known for certain why the horseshoe came to be an emblem of good luck. Some people suppose that it came from the old Norse worship of Thor, the Scandinavian god of thunder, to whom iron was sacred. But however the idea arose, the horse-shoe has always been regarded as lucky, and it is still in use with us today as a symbol of good luck.

Our ancestors believed that it had a potent power to keep witches at bay. John Aubrey (1626–97) took a great interest in antiquarian subjects and recorded that most houses in the West End of London had a horse-shoe nailed over the threshold. He relates that he even found one under the porch of a church once, and says that he was told of many similar instances. He adds sarcastically, according to John Brand in his *Popular Antiquities*, that 'One would imagine that holy water would have been sufficient.'

One can still find horse-shoes nailed up over the doors of old cottages in remote parts of the country—always with the points upwards, otherwise the luck they are supposed to bring will run out. If the shoe is to be really effective it is necessary that it should have been *found*, cast by a horse on road or field, not bought or given. Failing a lucky find, it was believed that the next best thing was to steal a shoe from the blacksmith's forge when the blacksmith was not looking. Such a shoe would be more effective than one freely given.

The colour and the markings of a horse have always been considered of importance, more especially by racing enthusiasts, who are often noted for their superstition over their favourite sport. A piebald horse is thought to be unlucky in England, though in some European countries the reverse opinion obtains. White horses are not looked upon with much favour, and older country people think it is unlucky to meet one when going to work in the morning, though they can annul the evil by spitting on the ground as they pass it. It can sometimes, however, be lucky to meet a white horse, for if one can think quickly enough to formulate a wish before seeing the animal's tail, the wish is sure to come true.

Black horses are considered to be fortunate, in Britain at least. Horses with white on their legs—stockings, those knowledgeable about horses call them—may or may not be desirable according to the legs on which the stockings appear. There is an old rhyme about horses with white stockings. It goes:

> One foot, buy me,
> Two feet, try me,
> Three feet, shy me,
> Four feet, fly me!

That, however, is not the end of it. Much depends upon which leg the one white stocking is. The best position is the near hind leg. If this is combined with a white star on the forehead, it should be a very lucky horse indeed, and those who bet on horse races should have no hesitation about backing it. The far hind leg is not so good, nor are the two front legs, but still they betoken good horses. Two white feet are also good if they are both on the fore-legs and if the white stockings are equal. The white must not come up too high, or the horse will be liable to stumble. Even on the lucky near hind leg, a white stocking that comes up too high reduces the luck a little.

A star of white on a horse's forehead is fortunate too, so long as it remains a star and does not cover so much of the forehead that it can be termed a white face. Should the white in a white-faced horse come down so low as to touch the nose, no horse-dealer in the past would have dreamt of paying a fair price for the animal. He might have bought it if he could have got it as a bargain, but if he had he would have got rid of it as soon as he had obtained an offer that would give him a small premium upon his money. Even today there are people who will fight shy of backing such a horse in racing, no matter how well it may have shaped in its trial gallops.

An old superstition about horses was that their owners, when eating eggs, should always eat an even number. If the number consumed was odd then it was thought that some evil would befall their stable. In Ireland this superstition was carried so far that grooms and stablemen were not allowed to eat eggs at all at one time. If by forgetfulness any had, they were made to wash their hands very thoroughly before touching either horse or harness.

Most people know of the white horses cut on the hill-sides of the chalk downlands in southern England. There are said to be seventeen of them in all, though only one of them is known to be of ancient origin. That one is the White Horse of Uffington, which was a familiar landmark at least as early as 1084, when mention was made of it in a charter belonging to Abingdon Abbey. It is almost certainly many centuries older than that. Legend says that it was cut by the order of King Alfred to celebrate his victory over the Danes, but some scholars think that it was probably made by the tribe of the Belgae, who inhabited southern England long before the Saxons and the Angles came. There is a super-stition attached to it by local people—if one stands in the centre of one of the horse's eyes and wishes, then the wish is sure to come true.

DOGS

SUPERSTITIONS about dogs are not so numerous as those about horses, but such as they are they are held very firmly by those who entertain them. Dogs are commonly supposed to have some kind of second sight, which enables them to see ghosts and, more usefully, to sense at once the true character of any stranger. They will, it is believed, greet the good man or woman with manifest pleasure, but will back away, growling, from a bad person. This is a widely-held opinion by many dog-owners. 'Dogs', they will tell you, 'always know.'

The howling of a dog has been considered an evil omen from very early times. It is usually supposed to foretell the death of some member of the family to which the animal belongs, or of a near neighbour. This belief was known in ancient Rome, where it had probably come from an even earlier age. Old country people still believe in it, despite much experience to the contrary. 'Dogs can scent death before it comes,' they assert. The only exception to this gloomy forecast is if the dog howls on a night when the moon is full. Then it is the bright moonlight which disturbs him, though long ago some credulous folk believed that he was howling in commiseration for his fellow-dog, the unfortunate creature who, legend says, was caught up to the moon along with his master, the Sabbath-breaker who was despatched there for picking up sticks on a Sunday. 'Sunday on earth or Monday in Heaven, 'tis all the same to me' this impious man is reputed to have said to the mysterious stranger who rebuked him for his sin. 'Is that so? Then keep an endless Moon Day in Heaven!' commanded the visitor, and forthwith the man and his dog ascended thither.

A dog heard howling at the time of the birth of a child was also looked upon as a bad sign. It did not necessarily foretell the early death of the infant, but it indicated that when he grew up he would lead an evil life. Shakespeare knew of this superstition. In *3 Henry VI* (v. vi. 41 ff.) King Henry says to Richard of Gloucester:

> Men for their sons', wives for their husbands',
> And orphans for their parents' timeless death,
> Shall rue the hour that ever thou wast born.
> The owl shriek'd at thy birth—an evil sign;
> The night-crow cried, aboding luckless time;
> Dogs howl'd, . . .
>
> To signify thou cam'st to bite the world.

Not so very long ago it was believed in some parts of Britain that if two people were engaged to be married and a dog ran between them as they walked together, it was a sign that the marriage would never take place. If it did then quarrels would occur and part the couple. If bride or bridegroom met a dog on the way to the wedding, it also foretold ill luck. However, in all these cases, if the threatened persons spat on the ground after the animal, misfortune would be avoided.

Dogs have their part in weather superstitions, some of which are still held to be reliable. When they eat grass, roll on the ground, or scratch themselves more than usual, it is said to be a sure sign that rain is coming. While, if it is a thunderstorm that is on the way, they can tell of its approach long before human beings are aware of it, and will cower under tables or in corners seeking safety.

CATS

In the history of superstition, the cat has held an important and enduring place. It was worshipped as a god in ancient Egypt; in Rome and Persia, if not actually worshipped, it was regarded with great esteem. The belief, still remembered in the old proverb 'a cat has nine lives', may have come partly from the reverence accorded to the animal in ancient days, combined with its known tenacity of life. This idea—that a cat could experience death eight times before a ninth demise finally put an end to its existence—may have been partly responsible for the cruelty with which cats were often treated in the past. Many of the pastimes in which our forebears indulged were concerned with the chasing and killing of cats. John Brand, in his *Popular Antiquities of Great Britain*, puts forward an idea which seems quite feasible—that the poor creature's persecutors maintained that the loss of two or three lives did not matter since it had so many at its disposal. The proverb is still in existence, but happily the belief is no longer acted upon in the blood-thirsty manner of the past.

Black cats now are usually considered to be luck-bringers, at least in Britain. Our ancestors, though, thought them unlucky, largely, no doubt, because of their reputation as the familiars of witches. With the departure of the dreaded Black Witch of the Middle Ages, amends have been made to the black cat, which is now regarded in this country as a bringer of good fortune. A stray cat coming to a house brings money in its train, if it is black. To stroke it brings good luck, while should a black cat cross a path or a road, the next person to go past will have a wish come true.

It is said that, in some countries, the reverse belief is held, so much so that some people starting out on a journey and seeing a black cat will turn round and go home again, fearing that they will encounter disaster if they continue on their way.

PIGS, SHEEP AND COWS

THE same idea, that it is unlucky to meet with one on beginning a journey, is applied to the pig in some parts of Britain, though it is not necessary to return home in order to avert the bad luck in the case of the pig. It is sufficient if one can contrive to pass it by walking or riding on ground on which the creature has not trod. To meet a sow with a litter of piglets beside her, however, is fortunate, for it indicates that the object of the journey will be successful. The sow met on her own is an unlucky omen.

To come across a flock of sheep or a herd of cows on the road is not considered a fortunate encounter in these days of motor vehicles, but our ancestors hailed it as a welcome omen—a superstition that probably had a good deal of reason behind it. In the days when the country was sparsely inhabited and the transport of food was costly and difficult, small communities were usually dependent upon their own efforts for the necessities of life. A flock of sheep or a herd of cattle seen approaching a village would mean meat and milk for the neighbourhood for a long time. One can see how this particular encounter would be thought fortunate in the past, and how it would survive as an omen of good luck long after the obvious significance of it was forgotten.

To see young lambs gambolling in a field was also accounted a good omen, probably for the same reason.

THE DONKEY

A donkey, of whatever sex, is commonly supposed to be an infallible weather prophet, being able to tell when rain is coming long before the meteorological office is aware of it. When wet weather is in the offing, the animal brays incessantly, warning farmers and outdoor workers of what they must expect. In addition to braying it keeps pricking up its ears, twitching them to and fro, and, even today, the old countryman often puts more reliance on these signs than on anything the official weather forecasts tell him.

There is an old legend about these same ears—'Ears like errant wings', as G. K. Chesterton calls them in his moving poem about the ass. The legend says that after Adam had been given the task of naming earth's creatures, as related in the Book of Genesis, the Lord God came down to walk in the Garden of Eden to hear the result of this nomenclatorial assignment. God spoke to each animal, one after the other asking what was the name it had been given, and, instructed by Adam, each creature answered promptly and correctly. Until it came to the turn of the donkey, who, despite his big head, possessed a very small brain and had forgotten his name completely. After the question 'What is your name?' had been put once or twice without eliciting any reply, Adam lost his temper. He seized the donkey by the ears, which until then had been of a moderate size, and pulled them unmercifully, crying out: 'Donkey! Your name is Donkey!' He pulled so hard that the animal's ears were lengthened considerably, and they have remained abnormally long ever since. It is because of this incident, the story says, that the donkey gained its reputation for stupidity.

Sometime during the Middle Ages, a superstition arose in Christendom that the markings on the donkey's back, which are roughly in the shape of a cross, only appeared after Christ's ride to Jerusalem on the first Palm Sunday. Thomas Browne mentions this belief in his *Pseudodoxia Epidemica: Enquiries Into Vulgar Errors*, though it is not clear whether or not he classed it as a 'vulgar error'. He says:

Common opinion ascribes this figure unto a peculiar signation; since that beast had the honour to bear our Saviour on his back.

He was a believer in witchcraft himself, so possibly he may have shared in this 'Common opinion'.

There is another belief about this mark which is of Jewish origin, and much older. It is that it resulted from Balaam's striking his ass on his way to Moab, as related in the Old Testament Book of Numbers, and that it appeared as perpetual reproof to him whenever he mounted the animal thereafter.

A popular belief about the donkey is that it always knows

when its death is near and goes away into some hidden spot to die alone—hence the saying 'One never sees a dead donkey.' On the rare occasions when a person *does* see one, great good luck is supposed to be in store for the seer.

THE GOAT

THE goat is an animal regarded by the superstitious with some uneasiness, an uneasiness which may possibly be a relic handed down from the ancient worship of the half-god, Pan, whose appearance according to pagan legend was very like that of a goat. When Pan was banished from the hierarchy along with the other Olympian gods at the coming of Christianity, the goat became associated with the Devil, who was supposed to take the form of this animal when he wished to appear anonymously on earth. This conception probably accounts for the medieval belief, mentioned by Sir Thomas Browne in his *Vulgar Errors*, that the devil has a cloven hoof on one of his feet. It would also account for the horns on his head as depicted in medieval drawings. The fact that a goat was used as a sin-offering in Jewish history, helped no doubt to foster this belief.

A superstition which was held by country people not so long ago, was that goats were never visible to mortal sight for twenty-four hours running. Sometime during that period they were said to disappear to visit their master, the Devil, in order to have their beards combed.

A goat's foot was commonly carried as a talisman to protect from the wiles of the Devil. Should such an object not be obtainable, a few hairs from the creature's beard served the same purpose.

RABBITS AND HARES

A TALISMAN which is often carried about by old country-men today is the foot of a hare or rabbit. The reasons given for this custom are various. 'To help my rheumatics' was one old man's explanation. 'It will give me good luck when shooting', said another. An old gardener explained his reason for carrying such an object as being that a hare's or rabbit's foot was the best possible implement with which to pollinate fruit blossoms; more especially peach blossom which, in our climate, is apt to come into flower while the weather is still too chilly for many pollinating insects to be about. A suggestion that a small paint brush with a long handle would do the trick as well, or even better, was treated with scorn. Every gardener knew that a hare's or rabbit's foot possessed some special quality that made a tree set fruit well.

It is rather curious that the feet of these two animals should be considered to make fortunate amulets, for, apart from their extremities, both of them are thought generally to be unlucky. A hare or rabbit crossing one's path was, in the past, enough to make one turn back and go home. It was certain that some evil would befall the traveller if the journey was continued after such a warning. Such an incident was regarded with concern if it occurred when bride and bridegroom were leaving the church after a wedding, for it was a sign that the marriage would be unhappy. Even our ancestors' favourite expedient of spitting was thought useless in this instance.

Another old belief concerning the hare was that if one was seen running along a street then some house that it had passed would be set on fire before much longer. In the old days a hare was seldom used for food, for it was believed that it caused melancholy in those who ate it. It is thought that this particular superstition probably dates back to a time before the Romans came to this country, for it is known that hares played a large part in the religious rites of the ancient Britons, and the animal was never eaten for food by the common people.

Apart from their feet, there is only one superstition attached to rabbits and hares that is favourable. If on the last day of the month, the last thing at night, upon getting into bed, a person says aloud 'rabbits', and on awakening says 'hares', before uttering anything else, he or she will receive a present before the month is over. Care must be taken, though, not to say anything after saying 'rabbits', otherwise the charm will not work and the effort is useless.

BATS

A BAT coming into the house is thought to be very unlucky for the whole household—illness, death, fire, loss of money, are only a few of the catastrophes variously prophesied as the result of such an untoward happening. This fear dates back at least as far as the time of the Roman poet Virgil, who lived from 70 to 19 B.C. He is said to have regarded these harmless creatures (except for the vampire, a blood-sucking bat found in Central and South America, they *are* quite harmless) with horror, and to have identified them with the winged monsters of Homeric legend.

RATS AND MICE

RATHER surprisingly, since both are so plentiful, not very

many superstitions are concerned with rats and mice. It is unlucky to have them in the house, but even a non-superstitious person might think that. To dream of them foretells a death, while if they should gnaw clothes or hangings it means loss of money. But this is a logical conclusion to draw from the occurrence, since clothes and curtains would probably have to be replaced, and money might well be said to be lost in consequence.

Birds and Insects

THERE can be hardly a bird in Britain to which some superstition has not at some time been attached. Some are lucky, some are unlucky, and they vary in different parts of the country, so that what is counted as unlucky in one part may well be considered lucky in another.

ROBINS

ONE familiar little bird, the robin redbreast, is a case in point. If, in some places, a robin should come into a house or peck against a closed window, it is thought to foretell a death in the household. But in other districts it is regarded as a harbinger of life—some unborn soul is about to be conceived by someone in the dwelling and the visitor is received with joy or sorrow according to circumstances. In all parts of the country, it is held to be very unlucky to kill a robin, and to feed it in cold weather, even at the risk of enticing it into the house, is an obligation if one hopes for good fortune. And everyone knows how it is not only cruel but downright disastrous to cage a robin:

> A Robin Redbreast in a Cage
> Puts all Heaven in a Rage,

Blake tells us in his poem, *Auguries of Innocence*. No one can possibly hope for good luck who does such a thing.

All these ideas about the robin probably stem from a belief once held in this country that if a robin came upon a dead body it then set to work to try to cover it with leaves and bits of moss. Some people think that the story of *The*

Babes in The Wood, which is now supposed to be *only* a story and not the narrative of some atrocious crime, may have given rise to this belief. Others maintain that the belief came first and suggested the theme of the story. Whichever way it was, the legend is an old one. Drayton, Shakespeare, Herrick, all mention this activity of the robin in their poems and plays.

In some parts of England a rather charming legend is told to account for the robin redbreast's habit of liking to keep close to some human dwelling, especially in winter time. It says that the little bird, out of its great compassion for suffering, takes every day a drop of water in its beak and flies as near as it can get to the underground regions in an attempt to quench the fires of hell. It has ventured so close to the fire that its feathers have become scorched, hence its red breast, and when it returns from its charitable mission it feels the cold much more than most birds after the fiery heat it has been through. So, if it can, it will slip inside some building to find shelter from the winter's blast.

This is a local legend, thought to have originated in Wales. A better-known, and much more widely-spread one, says that the robin's breast became red when the bird tried to pull out the thorns from the crown that encircled Christ's head at the Crucifixion and its feathers were stained with the blood of the Saviour, since which time all robins have had red breasts. With such a list of good deeds to its credit, it is not surprising that the bird is regarded with respect and affection, and that to kill it deliberately is thought to be a deed so evil that some terrible ill luck must assuredly befall the killer.

Nor was it only thought disastrous to kill the robin. The nest itself must be inviolate, as several old country rhymes tells us:

> The robin and the wren
> Are God Almighty's cock and hen.
> Him that harries their nest,
> Never shall his soul have rest!

And again:

> The robin and the redbreast,
> The robin and the wren,
> If ye take out o' their nest,
> Ye'll never thrive agen!

THE WREN

THE coupling of the robin and the wren together was due to an old belief that the wren was the robin's wife. But though the belief may have served to protect the wren's nest, the little bird itself was often treated with great cruelty. Hunting the wren was a sport followed in many parts of the British Isles as well as on the continent of Europe. Parties of men and boys, armed with sticks and stones, set out in quest of the tiny creature. When one had been started up it was pursued with cries and shouts and, if it was not nimble enough to escape, it was beaten to death. This practice was especially prevalent in the Isle of Man on certain days of the year (notably on Christmas Eve, on St Stephen's Day, and New Year's Day) and the inhabitants of the island had an old legend to justify it. There was once, they said, a fairy living there who had such great beauty that no male seeing her, could resist trying to embrace her. But she continually eluded their grasp, and led them step by step into the sea, where they perished. So many men did she dispose of in this way, that the islanders were afraid there would be none left to protect their shores against invasion. In this extremity a gallant knight came to the rescue. Resisting the lady's magical charms, he not only foiled her evil power, but evolved a plan to destroy her. She escaped destruction, however, by changing herself into a wren, and when she recovered her fairy form found herself invisible to human sight and so unable again to tempt men to their death. As a punishment for all the deaths for which she had been responsible she was condemned on one day every year to take again the shape of a wren. As a wren she could be seen by every one, and she was then pursued by angry crowds, intent upon killing her for fear lest she should at some future time regain her powers of enchantment. Since there was no way of distinguishing the fairy wren from the harmless birds, the zealous Manxmen killed all they could find. There was also a division of opinion as to which of the three special days was the one on which the sorceress was forced to become a bird, so they usually adopted all three for their national sport of Hunting the Wren.

The feathers of the slaughtered birds were considered potent to preserve those who carried them from drowning for the space of a year. It is said that they were much sought after in the past by fishermen and sailors, and by others who, for pleasure or profit, went to sea.

THE CUCKOO

THERE are many superstitions about the cuckoo, that summer visitor to our islands whose distinctive call is eagerly welcomed as a sign of spring. These are concerned mainly with hearing the call for the first time after the bird's arrival. It is considered to be unlucky to hear it first when one is lying in bed, but lucky if one is up and dressed, especially if one is out of doors. It is lucky to have money in one's pocket at the time; unlucky if one has none for it means that a year of poverty lies ahead. In Sussex it was thought to be especially lucky to hear a cuckoo for the first time if one was out of doors with cash in one's pocket on the fourteenth of April. For that day was known as Cuckoo Fair Day, the day when, according to Sussex legend, a bene-volent old woman let loose a cageful of cuckoos which she had fed and sheltered since the previous year.

The number of times a person hears the cuckoo call on the first occasion in spring was considered of great import-ance. A girl, hearing it, would ask aloud: 'Cuckoo, tell me true, when shall I be wed?' In reply the bird sings 'Cuckoo', as many times as there are years to pass before the event. Old people, weary of living, would ask when they would be relieved of their ills by death. The cuckoo is kept so busy answering all the questioners that it has no time, charitable people say, to build a nest during the mating season and so is obliged to lay its eggs in the nests of other birds.

It was once a custom for labourers, when they heard their first cuckoo, to down tools and make for the nearest inn to drink a 'Pint of Cuckoo Ale', as a toast to the summer visitor. It was also a custom for unmarried persons, both men and women, to take off a shoe—usually the left one—and look into it. If they were destined to be married there would be found a hair of the same colour as that of the future mate.

An old belief, no doubt to account for the disappearance of the cuckoo after its brief season, was that it turned into a sparrow-hawk during the winter and frequently remained in that form during the summer months. A still older belief was that the white frothy substance found on many plants in summer was the spit of the cuckoo. It is, as most people now know, made by an insect which encloses itself within it, cocoon-fashion, until it reaches maturity as a winged creature and flies away. The name cuckoo-spit is still given to the substance by country people.

The name 'cuckoo' figures a great deal in our country folk-lore. The wild arum, in addition to many other names, is known as Cuckoo-Pint because the cuckoo was supposed to sip water from it. Buttercups were sometimes called 'Cuckoo Buds', the silvery-mauve flowers found in damp meadows in spring, members of one of the cresses, Shakespeare's 'Lady-smocks all silver white', are known as cuckoo-flowers in some parts of Britain; and the pretty little white wood-sorrel is often termed Cuckoo's-meat from a belief that the cuckoo fed upon it.

Everybody knows that a deceived husband is called a Cuckold, a word derived from the Latin for cuckoo—unjustly so, most people think, since surely it should be the deceiver that bears the name? But not many are aware of a charm to use when carving a tough piece of meat. If it is found difficult, the carver is enjoined to 'think on a cuckold' by name, whereupon the knife in his hand will slice the joint easily. John Brand in his *Popular Antiquities of Great Britain* says that, according to an answer given to a query in a periodical of 1708, the charm was derived from a certain Thomas Webb: 'A carver to a Lord Mayor of London, in King Charles the First's reign was as famous for being a cuckold as for his dexterity in carving; therefore what became a proverb was used first as an invocation, when any took upon him to carve.'

The cuckoo usually leaves these islands in July, and though he sometimes stays on a little later

> In August
> Go he must.

It is said, though, that the bird has been seen in September, and there is an old English proverb that says:

> A cuckoo in September
> Is as much as the oldest man can remember,
> But see one in October
> 'Tis a thing he'll never get over.

A sure omen, apparently, of death!

UNLUCKY BIRDS

IF robins are lucky birds, and wrens and cuckoos mostly

harmless, the same cannot be said for many others of the species. Owls, magpies, and crows are definitely unlucky, though the ill luck is sometimes mitigated in particular circumstances. Two magpies, or two crows for instance, if seen together, foretell happiness:

> One crow sorrow,
>   Two crows mirth,
> Three crows a wedding,
>   Four crows a birth,
> Five crows silver,
>   Six crows gold,
> Seven crows a secret
>   Which never must be told!

Or dire consequences will follow for the viewer! A single magpie is very unlucky. There was a time when a country-man or woman, seeing a magpie at the start of a journey, would turn back, if it was at all possible to do so, for fear of some great disaster occurring should the expedition be continued. If it was not possible, various expedients were resorted to in an endeavour to ward off misfortune. In some parts of Britain it was customary for a man to raise his hat and ask politely: 'How is your wife?' A woman curtsied and made the same inquiry. Spitting could be helpful, as could also making the sign of the Cross, either on the breast or by crossing the thumbs. But whatever precautions were taken, our ancestors were definitely happier if magpies kept away from their part of the world.

Ravens were also dreaded, especially if one should perch on the roof of a house and croak when someone was lying ill inside. The bird was revered in ancient Greece and Rome as being possessed of prophetic wisdom. One, it is said, fluttered about the head of Cicero, the famous Roman orator, on the morning of the day when he met his death at the hands of his enemies—a sure sign that he was to come to disaster as he and all those who witnessed the occurrence believed. In Greece and Italy in pagan times, the bird was sacred to Apollo, and it was from the god, it was said, that its wisdom and fore-knowledge of events were received.

There was a tradition in Cornwall, still to be found in the last century, that King Arthur of Round Table fame, was alive in the form of a raven. Even when the birds became a nuisance many hesitated to shoot them, lest one of the victims should be the great warrior king. If Arthur finally died then he would not be available to come to the rescue, as the Middle Ages fervently believed that he would do, should Britain be in danger of being overwhelmed by her foes.

Rooks can be lucky or unlucky according to their behaviour. It is lucky for the owner of wooded property should a rookery be established in his trees, but definitely unlucky should the birds desert their nests and depart. They are reputed so to do when the last of a landed family dies leaving no heir. Considerately, they wait until the last owner is buried before they fly away to found a new colony elsewhere. Sometimes, though, 'smelling death approaching', they leave before it actually occurs, thereby giving warning of what is about to happen. They are also said to desert if a change of ownership is about to take place, due to the extravangance or the gambling debts of the owner. And they are reputed to have prescience of when the trees in which their nests are built are about to fall, and, long before any human being is aware of the danger, go to found a safer colony elsewhere.

Swallows, like rooks, are both lucky and unlucky. They herald good fortune when they build upon a house or barn or other edifice, but foretell ill luck when they leave. This is an old superstition and was obviously known to Shakespeare. In *Antony and Cleopatra* we are told that the augurers did not know what to make of it when swallows built their nests in Cleopatra's sails just before the final catastrophe. Shakespeare does not enlarge upon it, but his audience doubtless saw the implication, even though the augurers were puzzled. Swallows in their wisdom would not build upon an unsure foundation, so it would be obvious to those who watched the play that Cleopatra's barge would not again be required to move.

Of all the unlucky birds the owl is perhaps the chief, and the most dreaded. Superstition has nothing good to say of it. Its mournful cry foretells the death of someone, somewhere. Should it perch upon a building disaster will befall at least one of the persons within, while should it build its nest there, the place will be haunted by ghosts for the rest of its existence. Not until the last brick or stone has disappeared will the earthbound spirits leave the spot where the building once stood. It is said that consternation was once caused in ancient Rome when an owl strayed into the Capitol, the temple dedicated to the god Jupiter, and rites of purification had to be carried out before the building was allowed to be used for its normal purposes again. Even today, with the end of the twentieth century almost in sight, many people shiver superstitiously when they hear the hoot of an owl at night.

DOMESTIC FOWLS

DOMESTIC fowls, cocks, hens, ducks, geese, and peacocks, all have some superstitions attached to them, though except for peacocks and hens:

A whistling woman and a crowing hen
Are neither good for God nor men,

says an old rhyme—these do not betoken any evil. Mostly they indicate the kind of weather that may soon be expected. When a cock crows a great deal during the day, or when he and his harem of hens refuse to come out of the shed in which they roost at nights, it is a sign of rain on the way. The early morning crowing of a cock, though, was always a welcome sign to the countryman. Not only did it mean that the sun was about to rise and the darkness and dangers of the night were over, but it also meant that the ghosts who roamed the earth during the midnight hours would have to disappear. The crowing of the cock was the signal for their return to the underground world from which it was supposed they had emerged. This belief was a very old one. It has been traced back to ancient Roman times, and probably goes farther back still.

Another very old belief about the cock, one that continued into the sixteenth and seventeenth centuries if we may judge by the reference to it in Shakespeare's *Hamlet*, was that the bird crowed all through the hours of darkness on the night between Christmas Eve and Christmas Day, thus ensuring that no evil spirit might profane the earth during that holy time. For many reasons cock-crow seems to have been always welcome to our forefathers, even though the crowing kept them awake all night.

Should a hen take to crowing, however, it was a very different matter—as the rhyme already quoted denotes. It meant that the Devil had got into her and the only thing to do was to kill her as quickly as possible before she contaminated her companions. If she did no other harm, she would probably take to pecking and eating her eggs and teach the other hens to do the same. This belief still persists in some country places.

SWANS

THE swan, according to ancient Greek mythology, was one of the birds dedicated to Apollo, who, among other things, was the god of music. It is thought that this may have given rise to a belief, still held by some people, that swans sing when they are dying, though until then they make nothing but hissing noises. Another superstition still believed in about this bird is that it cannot hatch its eggs except in a thunderstorm. Swans sleep at night with their heads stretched back upon their folded wings, their long, sinuous necks enabling them to do this with ease. Should they take up this position during the day, as they do sometimes, the countryman confidently predicts that a thunderstorm will soon be coming.

DUCKS AND GEESE

THE countryman believes that he can foretell the weather from the behaviour of many birds, more especially from the aquatic birds such as ducks and geese. When they seem disturbed and hiss and quack more than usual, he says it is because they can sense wind and rain on the way. They know it is coming long before human beings do.

PEACOCKS

THE harsh cry of the peacock is also said to foretell rain, and there is an Arabian legend which purports to account both for this and for the beautiful bird's being always considered unlucky. The story says that it was the peacock who opened the gates of Eden and let in the Devil to spoil the innocence and happiness of Adam and Eve. As a punishment his once melodious call was changed to the unearthly shriek he emits now, in order, apparently, to warn Adam's descendants to take shelter from the inclement weather they would never have experienced had their ancestors been able to remain in paradise. The legend is little known in Britain, but the belief in the bird's ill luck is widely spread, and many people will not allow even one of its feathers to be brought into the house.

PIGEONS

PIGEONS are, on the whole, fairly harmless according to folk-lore, though our forefathers were rather uneasy if a white pigeon made a habit of settling upon a chimney of the house. In the days of feather beds there was a belief that the death agony was prolonged if there were any pigeon's feathers in the bed upon which the dying person was lying. Because of this belief, pigeon's feathers were usually burnt or buried after the bird was plucked for fear lest any should be included by unscrupulous people when stuffing beds and pillows.

BEES

OF all the insects known to man bees are perhaps the most important to his welfare, and it is natural that in a credulous, fear-ridden world, many superstitious ideas and practices should be concerned with them. Their industry, and their marvellously well-regulated existence have always excited interest, and the valuable product of their labours has caused them to be treated with almost reverential care.

Although their stings are very painful, they do not often employ them against human beings, nor do they appear to bear any malice towards the human race as long as they are treated respectfully. Superstition, however, says that they are very sensitive where their dignity is concerned, and there are certain rites which should be observed if there is to be harmony between them and their owners. It is thought that they take great interest in the doings of the households to which they belong, and they like to be informed of any unusual event which takes place—a birth, a death, a marriage, or the departure of one of the members to a foreign land. Especially do they like to know of a death in the family, and it is said that they will show their displeasure by deserting their hives if someone does not come at the earliest possible moment to tell them of the passing. During the last century it was even quite customary to place a piece of black *crêpe* upon the hive so that the intelligent little creatures could share in the mourning.

News of births and marriages also had to be communicated to the bees, and a piece of the christening or wedding cake was often laid before the entrance to the hive. Should this formality be omitted, or if nobody had the courtesy to come and tell them what was happening, it was believed that they would be so angry that they would sting the next member of the family they came across. They were apt to be angry, too, if when they swarmed their owner *gave* the swarm away. They thought that to be *given* away was derogatory to their dignity, as showing that they were regarded as creatures of little worth. A swarm must be duly paid for, and a proper price given for it, otherwise bad luck would come to both the giver and the person who received the gift.

This idea was sometimes carried to such an extreme that if bees swarmed at any distance from the original hive unless the owner collected them nobody else would do so until the owner had been traced and a fitting sale arranged. There is a church in a West Sussex village in which, some sixty years ago, a swarm of bees settled in the roof. The owner was unknown and for many decades the colony stayed there, growing bigger and bigger, until the dripping honey became a nuisance to the worshippers. At last a rector came to the living who refused to believe that ill luck would follow their removal, and, since nobody in the locality would undertake the work, a firm of 'outside' contractors was hired to clear the church of the insects. Within a year of this 'sacrilege', as the older villagers regarded it, the rector had a stroke in the vestry one morning, just before a service, and died. Everyone knew why!

Not long after this, a swarm of bees settled in a chimney of a house in the same village. Where the swarm had come from nobody knew. No one came to claim it, and though there were one or two ardent beekeepers in the neighbourhood not one of them would touch it. Remembering the rector's fate no one—beekeeper, sweep, or local builder—would come to the rescue. Everyone remembered how the late rector had had the bees removed from the church, 'And look what happened to him!' was the universal rejoinder to the pleas of the chimney's owner. It was the kitchen chimney, where a fire in an all-the-year-round range was burning, and overcome by the fumes all the unfortunate insects perished.

This was in the present century, not much more than twenty years ago.

In some places, though bees must not be given away, it is considered unlucky to pay for them in actual coin, unless the coin in question is gold. If gold cannot be obtained, as nowadays is the case, then a load of hay or some trusses of corn would be considered in exchange for a swarm. An old country proverb confirms this:

> A swarm of bees in May
> Is worth a load of hay;
> A swarm of bees in June
> Is worth a silver spoon;
> A swarm in July
> Is not worth a fly!

SPIDERS

SPIDERS have a great many superstitious beliefs attached to them. It is very unlucky to kill a spider.

> If you wish to live and thrive
> Let the spider run alive

says the proverb, and there is no doubt that the belief has been held by the credulous for many centuries. It can be traced back to an old Greek legend. A certain Athenian maid, named Arachne, excelled in the art of weaving, and she was so proud of her skill that she was rash enough to challenge the goddess Athena to a contest, to see which of them could weave the finest piece of cloth. The maid had not underrated her own ability, and her piece of weaving was so much the superior that the goddess flew into a rage and tore it to bits. Frightened and distressed, Arachne attemped to hang herself. Athena prevented her from doing that, but she was still angry, and to show her displeasure she turned the unfortunate girl into a spider. Arachne's skill in weaving was transmitted to her descendants, and spiders have spun the most beautiful and intricate webs ever since, while they are able to hang from threads for hours on end without harming themselves.

The vengeful goddess seems to have had some qualms of conscience about her jealous action, for she is said to have taken the little creatures under her protection, to visit bad luck upon those who hurt them, and to reward with good health those who allow them to live unmolested in their dwellings. There may have been good ground for the belief that spider-infested houses were healthy in the dark and dirty Middle Ages. For spiders prey upon flies, the carriers of many diseases, and there would certainly have been far fewer flies in a house full of spiders. There may be, too, some truth in the old idea that a spider's web laid upon a cut helped to heal it by congealing the blood. It may also act as some kind of antibiotic. Bottom evidently thought so in *A Midsummer Night's Dream.*

The little red spiders, usually plentiful in this country, are thought to denote money coming to the person upon whose clothing they alight. Should there be a thread attached to this money-spider's body, the loose end of it should be taken up and the spider swung carefully three times round the head of the person in question. This will ensure that the lucky omen will be fulfilled.

CRICKETS

ANOTHER insect which it is thought to be bad luck to kill is the cricket, the brown-coloured, little jumping creature which is allied to the grasshopper. In the days of old-fashioned, wide-open fireplaces, a cricket often came into a house and took up its residence in some chink or recess in the bricks at the base of the chimney, whence it could be heard making a kind of chirping noise, usually at night. To have a cricket in one's house was considered to be very fortunate. If, after some years' residence, it suddenly departed, then much concern was felt by the household, for it was believed that the little creature knew that some disaster was on the way, and had decided to leave before it became involved in the trouble.

SOME OTHER FLYING INSECTS

LADYBIRDS are definitely lucky, they bring money in their train. So are flies if they fall into the glass from which anyone has been drinking. The crane-fly, commonly known as Daddy-Long-Legs, is also lucky, and should never be killed. Nor should glow-worms, for their light in the vicinity of a dwelling protects the house and its inmates from harm. Wasps, as one might expect, can be destroyed with impunity. No ill can come from killing them, even if no great good, except in the case of the first wasp seen in the spring. If that is killed, the killer will have good luck and will not be troubled by enemies during the year.

Rather strangely, since it is such a beautiful and distinctive insect, the dragonfly seems to have little superstition attached to it. Children, however, credit it with one magic power—it can distinguish a good boy from a bad one. When a good boy goes fishing, the dragonfly will hover over the stretch of water where the fish are plentiful so that, if he follows the lead thus given, the lad will have a fine catch. But if the boy is bad it will be useless for him to try to take advantage of the sign, for the dragonfly, sensing his badness, will lead him to water where there are no fish at all.

The Vegetable Kingdom

PLANTS of every kind have always figured largely in the folk-lore of all countries, as we know from the legends concerning them that have come down to us from the past. Much of the superstition still attached to our trees and flowers, shrubs, fungi, and other vegetable growths can be traced back beyond the days of ancient Greece and Rome.

THE HOLLY

Of all the trees are in the wood,
The holly bears the crown,

says the well-known carol. It also has more superstition woven about it than any other of our British arboreal plants. The tree is considered entirely good; its very name is a corruption of the word 'holy'. It plays a large part in Christian symbolism. Its evergreen leaves are an emblem of eternal life; its red berries are said only to have become that colour after the Crucifixion, and its prickly leaves make it impossible for devils or witches or other evil creatures to touch it.

It was as a preventive of witchcraft that our ancestors most valued the holly. Witches and wizards fought shy of houses guarded by holly trees, and sprays of holly brought indoors at Christmas time helped to keep the premises free of these noxious persons. Even today there are people who like to have at least one sprig of berried holly in every room of the house, though they probably have no fear, or thought, of witches. But belief in the potency of holly as a charm

still lingers subconsciously in the collective mind, and it is not only for the beauty of its leaves and berries that it is so much in use as a Christmas decoration—there is a vague feeling that it will bring good luck to the household as well.

Holly bushes may be seen in many woods and fields today. The plant is indigenous in Britain and it may be growing naturally wild, but it is also possible that it marks the site of some old dwelling, long since vanished, whose inhabitants had planted holly trees to keep the dreaded witches away.

In some countries an infusion of holly leaves is sprinkled upon the foreheads of newborn infants—to keep away evil spells. It was probably for this same reason that carters, in the days when horses played such a large part in farm work and in transport, liked to have their whip handles made of holly wood. John Evelyn, who lived from 1620 to 1706, believed that coal might be found below the soil where hollies grew abundantly, and this belief can still be met with in some country places in Britain, though there seems to be no record of anyone's ever having put the theory to the test.

Nicholas Culpeper, the famous herbalist who lived from 1616 to 1654, recommends eating the berries of the holly in his *Complete Herbal*. A dozen of them, he says, eaten in the morning fasting 'when they are ripe and not dried, they purge the body of gross and clammy phlegm'. Modern pharmacists, however, would not look with favour upon this remedy. They consider the berries to be slightly poisonous, causing such violent sickness and diarrhoea that they can even be dangerous to life. Anyone wishing to try their efficacy now would do better to try another recipe advised by the old herbalist; to use, that is, the bark and leaves of the tree in fomentations to heal broken bones and 'such members as are out of joint'. Whether or not such fomentations had any effect upon broken bones and dislocated joints at least they probably did not do much harm if gently applied.

THE ELDER

THE elder was another tree which was regarded as affording some protection against witches. But it had not the holy virtues attributed to the holly. Legend says that it was the tree from which Christ's cross was made, and also that it was the one upon which Judas hanged himself in his penitence.

These ideas gave it a reputation that made the unlettered countryman in the past regard it with respectful awe. It is said that when it was necessary to cut down an elder tree, the woodman knelt down on the ground before it and asked its pardon for what he was about to do. Should he fail to pay the tree this respect, ill luck would come to him. Although this practice no longer persists, relics of it may still be found in the reluctance among country people to use elder wood for burning.

It is possibly due to the above legends that a belief is held in many country villages that an elder tree is never struck by lightning.

Old countrymen believe that leaves of the elder placed in mole runs will drive away moles. An old home-made insecticide was made from infusing the flowers in water and pouring the liquid over fruit trees, a somewhat useless effort one might imagine. Culpeper says that a decoction of the juice of the roots 'cures the bite of an adder and the bites of mad dogs', while the 'juice of the leaves snuffed up into the nostrils, purges the tunicles of the brain', and the 'juice of the berries boiled with honey and dropped into the ears, helps the pain of them'. He also recommends distilled water of the flowers to cleanse the skin from sunburn, freckles and the like. Gerard, too, who died in the year that Culpeper was born, was fervent in his praise of the medicinal virtues of the elder. John Evelyn, born four years after Culpeper died and who lived on into the eighteenth century, described the tree as 'a kind of Catholicon against all infirmities whatever'.

THE ASH

THERE was a superstitious custom practised once in

Britain, in connection with the ash tree, which has now, fortunately, entirely disappeared. It was concerned with the treatment of rupture in children and for children suffering from rickets. A young ash tree was split open perpendicularly, then, while the two sides were held apart the child to be treated was stripped and passed through the aperture made by the cut. After this part of the operation had been accomplished, the two sides of the trunk were brought together again, the cuts were plastered with soil, and bound tightly together with strips of material. The tree would be left bandaged like this for a prescribed period, varying in different parts of the country, and then unbound. If the cut parts had adhered then it was supposed that the patient would eventually be cured. If, however, there was still a gap between them, it was considered that the treatment had failed.

Should the ash tree die, or be cut down, the ill from which the child had suffered would return, even though he had seemed to have outgrown it, and no matter how long it was since the operation had taken place. Many villages in England have ash trees—or hawthorn trees which were sometimes used for the same purpose—which show by the malformation of their trunks that they have been used in this way.

A one-time superstition about the ash was that it was lucky to find a leaf where the smaller leaflets of which it was composed were even in number, such being usually uneven. If one *was* found the finder picked it, and holding it in his hand made a wish, saying the moment he had done so:

> Even ash I thee do pluck,
>> Hoping thus to meet good luck.
> If no luck I get from thee,
>> I'll wish I'd left thee on the tree.

The wish was then supposed in due course to be fulfilled.

An even ash leaf was also used as a charm to tell a young woman which of her male acquaintances would be her future husband. If she placed an even ash leaf under her pillow at night, she would see in her dreams the man she was destined to marry. A young man could use the same charm to dream of his future wife.

THE OAK

THE oak tree has always been of great importance in Britain. The Druids seem to have regarded it with reverence, and later ages have esteemed it for its usefulness. It was of enormous use in building, more especially for ships, and at one time its fruit was the staple food for rearing pigs. As one might expect, in addition to its many practical uses, there were superstitious traditions gathered around it. One, which it shares with the ash tree, is half-believed to this day—that the weather of the coming summer may be told from the burgeoning of it in spring.

> If the ash is out before the oak
> Then we're going to have a soak!
> But if the oak's before the ash
> Then we'll only get a splash.

Most people's experience is that, in England, the oak is always in leaf before the ash tree begins even to think about it. Yet every year one usually hears the old rhyme quoted hopefully, despite the fact that we can almost always expect the 'soak'.

The galls (commonly known as oak-apples) which are made by insects, and often found on oak trees, especially upon young ones, were the cause of much speculation to our ancestors. They were used mainly for divination. Thomas Lupton, whose exact dates seem not to be known but who flourished sometime in the fifteen-hundreds, published a work entitled *A Thousand Notable Things of Sundry Sortes*, in which he explains how to read the oak-apple oracle:

> If you take an oak-apple from an oak tree, and upon the same you shall find a little worm therein, which if it doth flye away it signifies wars; if it creeps, it betokens scarceness of corn; if it run about, then it foreshews the plague. This is the countryman's astrology, which they have observed for truth.

A slightly different version of this prognostication says that a fly found inside the oak-apple denotes war; a spider, pestilence; a small worm, plenty.

THE HAWTHORN

ONE of the most firmly-held superstitions about trees is that pertaining to the hawthorn, or may tree. Our forefathers believed that it was fatal to bring mayflowers into a house. The death of one of the inhabitants, they said, was sure to follow such a foolish act before a year was out. The fact that it seldom did occur never seemed to shake belief in the omen, and to this day few people are brave enough to bring the hawthorn's flowers indoors. Why the tree should have acquired this sinister reputation for its blossom it is difficult to say, for in all other respects it is considered to be a plant of virtue. Legend says that from its thorns was composed the crown Christ wore upon the Cross, and that it is from grief of this use being made of it that it now bears its autumn crop of blood-red berries—in memory of the blood that once bedewed that sacred head. It was, the legend goes on to say, from the thorns of this crown that Joseph of

Arimathea planted a hedge which grew so quickly—owing to the holy blood still upon them—that he was able to cut a strong staff from one of the bushes to take with him on his journey to Britain, the staff which is said to have burst into leaf and blossomed on Christmas Day, to convince the heathen inhabitants of these islands that the Gospel story the saint had brought to them was true. It is this same bush that is still supposed to flower at Christmas—or rather *would* still do so, superstition says, had not the powers-that-be altered the calendar in 1752, which so confused the poor tree that it gave up its winter flowering for ever.

But though it no longer flowers at Christmas, the hawthorn still possesses many virtues. It knows when the danger of frost is over in Spring, and never opens its blossoms until it is certain that no more is to come, thus informing men when it is safe for them to discard their winter clothing.

> Cast not a clout
> Till may be out,

says the old proverb, and though there is some argument as to whether the month of May or the hawthorn flower is meant, the true believer has no doubt about it. It is the flower that the proverb refers to, for the hawthorn tree with its magical foreknowledge *knows*.

THE HAZEL OR NUT-TREE

THE hazel tree has a virtue ascribed to it which may or may not be superstition. It is the tree from which the rods are cut that the water-diviner uses for his divination. A forked shoot is taken from a young hazel, and the diviner, holding the ends of the fork in his hands, walks slowly backwards and forwards over the ground where he hopes to find an underground spring for a well. Should he come upon one then the third end of the rod bends downwards and indicates the spot where the well should be dug.

This divination certainly works with some operators, though whether it is due to the hazel rod itself or to some special sensitivity in the diviner is not certain. It is claimed by some that buried gold may be located in the same way. It used to be thought that the divination was only successful if carried out on Midsummer's Eve, and that a secret incantation had to be muttered under the breath while the operation was in progress. This part of it, of course, was pure superstition, but the ordinary use of the hazel rod has had many successful results to justify the practice. It is probable, however, that the faculty lies in the operator and not in the hazel twig, and that a shoot of the right shape and flexibility from any tree would do as well.

The hazel rod, however, is the one most widely used today, and since the practice of water-divining is very ancient—the Chaldeans are said to have practised it, and the Old Testament tells us that Moses found water for the Israelites in the desert by means of a rod—it is very likely that it was a shoot from a hazel tree which was always most favoured by a diviner. Tradition dies hard, and may persist through many centuries.

THE APPLE

As far back in time as we can trace, the apple has been regarded as a most important fruit. In the legends of the Norse gods, it was by eating the apples of the tree that grew in the gardens of Asgard that the gods retained their strength and youth, and throughout history apples have been considered to be bringers of health to those who eat them regularly.

> An apple a day
> Keeps the doctor away,

says a well-known proverb and one rather less well-known but to the same effect announces:

> Eat an apple on going to bed,
> And you'll keep the doctor from earning
> his bread.

So important did our ancestors think the apple, that they carried out semi-religious rites at certain seasons which they believed would help the trees to flourish and bear good crops. On Twelfth Night, in particular, it was customary for the apple-grower and his labourers to gather round the best apple-trees in the orchard, where with songs and supplications they begged the genii that guarded the trees to make them grow well and set much fruit during the coming year. This ancient rite degenerated into a noisy revel as time went on, but in its debased form it continued in some places into the early years of the present century. The men gathered as of old round the trees, laughing and shouting and drinking beer and cider, and singing a doggerel rhyme, which usually ran on lines similar to the following:

> Here's to thee,
>   Old Apple-tree,
> Whence may'st bud,
>   Whence may'st blow,
> And whence thou may'st bear
>   Apples enow!
> Hats full! Caps full!
>   Bushels and sacks full!
> And my pockets full, too!
>   Huzza!

After which a mug of cider was usually flung over at least one of the trees so serenaded to encourage it to bring forth the fruit that goes to make the delectable drink.

In some parts of the country, there is a superstition that should an apple tree bear blossoms out of season when the fruit is ripe, it means a death in the family of the owner of the orchard. On the other hand many people say that this phenomenon means good fortune for the owner. Most children are familar with the custom of throwing the peel of an apple over the left shoulder to discover whether or not they will be married when they grow up. If the peel, which must be in one piece from the whole of the apple, breaks in the process then the thrower will never be married. If it remains unbroken it means marriage, and the shape it takes as it lies on the ground indicates the initial letter of the future spouse's name.

Another method of divination is to take an apple pip between the finger and thumb and to walk round in a circle squeezing it, at the same time repeating aloud:

> Pippin, pippin, paradise,
> Tell me where my true love lies.

Whereupon the pip is supposed to burst and shoot its pith, north, south, east, or west, in the direction in which the future lover lives. These superstitious customs are only children's games now, but they seem once to have been taken seriously by grown-up people.

NUTS, PEACHES AND PEARS

NUTS, as we have seen, were largely used for fortune-telling in the past (page 39). The countryman believed, also, that nut trees were good weather prophets. A big crop of nuts meant a hard winter, a poor crop, the winter would be mild. A prediction allied to this was that a good crop of walnuts, besides prophesying a hard winter, promised a fine corn harvest in the next year. If peach and pear leaves fall in summer, before their due time, cattle disease will follow very shortly. And there is a popular belief that no man who plants pear trees can ever hope to eat of their fruit—they take too long to come into bearing.

> Who plants pears
> Plants for his heirs,

runs the old saying, which may be the reason why so few gardens these days have pear trees in them, though there are plenty of apple and plum trees. Gardeners, it seems, are not so altruistic as they were once upon a time.

GORSE

GORSE, or furze as it is sometimes called, is said to be unlucky if it is brought into a house as a decoration. But its flowers were much used by the old herbalists in their decoctions, and apparently no ill consequences followed bringing it indoors for purely medicinal purposes. The potion made from it was said to be good for jaundice and for all kidney and liver troubles. It is rather curious that it should have been considered unlucky, in view of the old country proverb which declares that:

> Kissing's out of season
> When gorse is out of bloom—

that is to say never, since there is not a month in the year when a flower or two may not be found on a gorse bush somewhere in these islands.

THE LAUREL

THERE are many species of laurel and many were the virtues ascribed to them all in bygone days. Culpeper has much to say about the bay variety of laurel.

> It is a tree of the Sun, and under the celestial sign Leo, and resisteth witchcraft very potently, as also all evils old Saturn can do the body of man, and they are not a few: for it is the speech of one, and I am mistaken if it were not Mizaldus, that neither witch nor devil, thunder nor lightning, will hurt a man where a bay tree is . . . the berries are very effectual against all poisons of venomous creatures, and the sting of wasps and bees, as also against the pestilence or other infectious diseases. . . . The oil made of the berries is very comfortable in all cold griefs of the joints, nerves, arteries, stomach, belly, or womb; and helpeth palsies, convulsions, cramp, aches, trembling and numbness in any part, weariness, also, and pains that come by sore travailing. All griefs and pains proceeding from wind, either in the head, stomach, back, belly or womb, by anointing the parts affected therewith; and pains of the ears are also cured by dropping in some of the oil. . . . The oil takes away the marks of the skin and the flesh by bruises, falls, etc, and dissolveth the congealed blood in them. It helpeth also the itch, scabs, and weals in the skin.

No wonder so many old gardens are girt about with hedges of this wonderful shrub and that laurel leaves were used to crown the victors in the old Olympic games of Greece and Rome. It was considered by the ancient Greeks and Romans that the laurel, or daphne, was under the special protection of the sun god Apollo and there was an attractive legend to account for this. The god loved a beautiful maiden, named Daphne, but was so ardent in his pursuit of her that she fled from him in alarm, and calling upon the other gods for help was changed into a laurel tree, greatly to the grief of her lover. Thereafter he wore a wreath made of the leaves of the plant, and, since Apollo was also the patron of athletes, set the fashion for rewarding the victor in war or in more peaceful pursuits with a crown of laurel.

NETTLES AND DOCKS

NETTLES and docks are commonly found growing together, and country people in the past believed that this was by a special dispensation of providence, so that those who were stung by the nettle might find immediate relief by rubbing the stung parts with a dock leaf, the juice of which certainly does have a slightly soothing effect. This effect, the superstitious say, is enhanced if one repeats the following charm while rubbing:

> Dock in, nettle out!
> Dock rub nettle out!

Anne Pratt, in her attractive book, *The Flowering Plants, Grasses, Sedges and Ferns of Great Britain*, mentions this widely-held belief, but dismisses it rather summarily by saying: 'The expressed juice of the honeysuckle leaf, is a far more efficacious remedy against the sting either of plant or insect than the Dock-leaf, the sole virtue of which seems to consist in its coolness.' She admits, however, that this coolness makes the leaf useful for wrapping around butter and says that because of this use the plant is often called the Butter dock, to distinguish it from others of the species.

Old countrymen believe that docks will only grow in good and fertile soil, and that a wise farmer will never buy or rent a farm on which no docks are found.

Nettles are said to have been brought to this country by the Romans, who used them to warm their cold limbs, half-frozen in our chilly climate. Whether they really indulged

135

in such an heroic practice is doubtful, but tradition holds firmly that they did, and one of the species is still known as the Roman nettle. The sting of the plants is said to be good for the aches and pains of rheumatism and sciatica, and the old herbalists found many other medicinal uses for them. A drink made from the seeds cured the bites of mad dogs (how frequently dogs seem to have gone mad in the sixteenth and seventeenth centuries!) and was a remedy for the poisonous qualities of hemlock, henbane, nightshade, mandrake, or 'such herbs as stupify the senses'—according to Culpeper.

THE BRAMBLE

A CURIOUS practice, in use in the last century, was recommended by country folk to do away with blackheads, often a troublesome complaint of young people. An arched bramble was sought for, that is, one that had a branch spreading out from the parent plant and rooting at a short distance so as to form an arch. This found, the sufferer was instructed to crawl through the arch on hands and knees three times, going, of course, the way of the sun from east to west. If the cure was to work successfully, he—or she—must pass through the arch without a scratch or getting the clothes torn.

A superstition that survives to some extent to this day is that once Michaelmas Day is past blackberries, the fruit of the bramble, are injurious to the health of those that eat them. People may not now believe, as their forebears did, that the Devil had taken possession of the berries since St Michael, who had hitherto protected them from the archenemy, was now too occupied with other matters to look after them. But one may still be warned against eating them when September is over on the grounds that they are no longer fit for food at this time of the year.

THE MANDRAKE

THE mandrake, a member of the potato family, is not indigenous in Britain, but it is occasionally found in old gardens, for it was much valued by the herbalists of the Middle Ages for use in their medicines. It was also regarded with a great deal of awe, for it was supposed to possess some human qualities, and it was believed that it screamed aloud when it was pulled from the soil in which it grew. It was dangerous to the person who ventured to pull it up and to avoid the danger an elaborate method of extracting the root, the part of the plant mostly desired, was resorted to. Having dug carefully around it to loosen the earth, the would-be gatherer tethered a dog, a black one for preference, to the exposed part with a strong cord. A tempting piece of meat was then held out to the animal just beyond its reach. In its eagerness to seize the meat the dog would bound forward and drag the mandrake out of the ground. The dog was then supposed to die. The operator had to be careful to stop up his ears before commencing work, lest he too should die or be driven mad by the sound of the fearful shriek the plant was believed to emit.

Once in the hands of the herbalist—or a witch—the root was put to innumerable uses. Sometimes it was carved to resemble a puppet and sold for a high price to a childless woman, when it was supposed that she would conceive. John Donne (1572-1631) refers to this belief in one of his poems:

> Go and catch a falling star,
> Get with child a mandrake root.

There is also a reference to it in Genesis 30:14–16.

Other uses for it were as a purgative and an emetic; it was credited with curing goitres, boils, erysipelas, and many other diseases. It was also considered to be a powerful narcotic, as Shakespeare knew. He makes mention of this atribute of the mandrake in some of his plays, notably in *Othello*, where he makes the treacherous Iago say of the master he has deceived:

> Look where he comes! Not poppy, nor mandragora,
> Nor all the drowsy syrups of the world,
> Shall ever medicine thee to that sweet sleep
> Which thou ow'dst yesterday.

He knew, too, about the dreadful shriek the plant was supposed to give when torn from the ground, and refers to it in both *Romeo and Juliet* and in *The Second Part of Henry VI*.

CLOVER

IN contrast to the awe with which the mandrake was regarded, clover has always enjoyed a happy and beneficent reputation. 'He's in clover', is said of a person enjoying good fortune, an allusion to the enjoyment of cattle when feeding in clover fields. And everyone knows of the good luck attached to finding a four-leaved clover:

> You must search the meadows over
> Till you find a four-leaved clover:
> Fortune then will smile on you,
> Make your dearest wish come true.

While another rhyme says:

> If you find a four-leaved clover
> You'll see your love ere day is over.

Sir John Melton, who lived in the time of Elizabeth the First, James the First, and Charles the First (he died in 1640) seems to have been a believer in the luck of a clover leaflet with four leaves, for he says in his *Astrologaster:*

> If a man, walking in the fields, finds any four-leaved clover grass, he shall, a short while after, find some good thing.

Nor was it only the four-leaved variety which was prized by our forefathers. They knew, as we know, that any sort of clover made excellent food for cattle, and that, a factor which must have appealed to them greatly, it was a powerful protection against witchcraft.

THE SNOWDROP

ONE might have thought that the snowdrop, the lovely little flower so loved and looked for in our hemisphere in January and February, would also have been looked upon as a bringer of good luck. But not so! It has an unfortunate superstition attached to it. Although welcome in the garden it should never be brought into the house, more especially if there should be a sick person in the dwelling. If it is, the illness will prove fatal. In some parts of Britain this belief is modified a little—death results only if a child brings the flower indoors. Yet this idea about the snowdrop may not, perhaps, appear so strange if one thinks a little. Snowdrops flower at a time of the year when illness is very prevalent, and many suffering from some forms of it may die. It is customary to take flowers to the sick, and during these winter months not many flowers are about. Snowdrops may often have been brought to patients who afterwards have died. To the superstitious mind, apt to find omens in everything, the two events may have seemed to be connected, and so the snowdrop has become saddled with the reputation of being a harbinger of death.

VIOLETS, ROSES AND LILIES

ALTHOUGH it is safer not to take snowdrops or any *white* flower into a house where there is sickness, just in case the patient or family believe in the superstition, violets, roses, and any coloured lilies are welcome gifts. Red roses, as everybody knows, carry love with them. Violets show good will on the part of the giver and are much appreciated if the owner of the house into which they are taken keeps chickens or ducks. They will bring good fortune upon the broods of ducklings and chicks. Lilies of the valley, although they are white, may be given as long as plenty of their green sheaths are brought in with them. It is, however, thought to be unlucky to plant lilies of the valley oneself. If one wants them in the garden, it is best to get somebody else to put them in the ground for you.

PARSLEY AND MINT

PARSLEY and mint are highly desirable herbs to have in the garden because of their usefulness in cooking, but superstition has made it hard for the gardener to get them established. Roots of them should not be given away—it was an insult to the guardian genius of the mint and parsley beds to do so, and misfortune would come to the family of the giver if he disregarded the threat. One could sow them, but neither plant was likely to come up unless the seed was sown on Good Friday, and only then if the sun was shining and the weather mild. Moreover, it was dangerous for a *woman* to sow parsley unless she wanted a child. 'Sow parsley, sow babes', said an old proverb, a proverb that was certainly believed in by some countrywomen less than half a century ago.

No special evil followed the sowing of mint, but it simply refused to come up unless the person who sowed it was destined to be wealthy. In that case it might germinate and flourish, but since the vast majority of us are condemned, if not to poverty, to only moderate means, a good crop of mint from sown seed is rare indeed. It seems that the only sure way to get mint into one's garden is to steal a few roots from some unsuspecting friend or neighbour.

MOONWORT

A curious superstition, no longer held but one widely believed in a couple of centuries ago, is concerned with the moonwort—a small plant usually classified with the fern tribe, found on moors and commons in most parts of the British Isles. It gets its name from the shape of the leaflets on its fronds, which are definitely the shape of half-moons, and it is said to have the power to pick locks and to act as a magnet to draw off the shoes from a horse's hooves. William Cole (1626–62) says:

> It is said, yea, and believed by many, that moonwort will open the locks where-with dwelling-houses are made fast, if it be put into the key-hole; as also that it will loosen the locks, fetters, and shoes from those horses' feet that goe on the places where it groweth; and of this opinion was Master Culpeper, who, though he railed against superstition in others, yet had enough of it himselfe, as may appear by his story of the Earl of Essex his horses, which being drawn up

in a body, many of them lost their shoes upon White Downe in Devonshire, near Tiverton, because moonwort grows upon heaths.

George Wither, or Withers as his name is sometimes spelt, a minor poet writing in 1622, says of the plant in his work *Abuses Stript and Whipt*,

> There is an herb, some say, whose vertue's such
> It in the pasture, only with a touch,
> Unshoes the new-shod steed.

Guillaume de Saluste Du Bartas, a French poet who lived in the sixteenth century, wrote some lines about this plant which have been roughly translated into English by Joshua Sylvester (1563–1618). They show that the superstition was not confined to Britain.

> And horses that, feeding on the grassy hills,
> Tread upon moonwort with their hollow heels,
> Though lately shod, at night go barefoot home,
> Their masiter musing where their shooes become.
> O moonwort! Tell us where thou hidst the smith,
> Hammer, and pincers, thou unshod'st them with,
> Alas! What lock or iron engine is't
> That can thy subtile secret strength resist,
> Sith the best farrier cannot set a shoe
> So sure, but thou (so shortly) canst undo?

There were, however, doubters even in those credulous years. In *The British Physician*, a work published by Turner in 1687, the author says confidently that though moonwort 'be the moon's herb, yet it is neither smith, farrier, nor picklock'—which dictum may have brought some comfort to the riders of his day.

Remedies and Charms

A MID all the dangers which they believed surrounded them,
it is not surprising that our ancestors clutched at anything
which they supposed might protect them from the devils,
witches, hobgoblins, ghosts, and other malevolent beings
who, they imagined, were continually lying in wait to do
them harm.

Of the numerous menaces, perhaps that from the Devil troubled them the least. After all, the Church afforded some protection from him—at any rate for the God-fearing man. The church building offered sanctuary, once one had passed safely through the peril from the ghosts and evil spirits that might lurk in the graveyard. Church bells, too, were potent against such creatures, and it was possible to buy Indulgences from the priests which would save one from the worst pains of purgatory. And even after the Reformation had made it impossible to obtain Indulgences in England, one could still obtain favoured treatment after death by present-ing the local church with a set of Communion Plate, or a pair of silver candlesticks. Even those too poor to be able to afford such handsome offerings could get some remission from their sins by attending church services regularly, and making long prayers.

But witches were uninterested in Communion Plate and candlesticks, nor did the priests offer much help where witchcraft was concerned. Even when the Church itself was going through its most superstitious stage, it frowned upon any dealings with witches. To guard against their machin-ations, people were mostly left to their own devices. Our forefathers turned to all kinds of expedients to try to prevent the sorcerer's spell from operating, or, if too late to prevent it, to find some remedy to cure the evil.

As we have seen, growing special trees and plants around a dwelling relieved its inmates of much of their fear regard-ing dangers at home. But it was not possible for them always to stay at home within the protective guard of holly, laurel, and other friendly growths. It was often necessary to go abroad, and then the carrying of some amulet was—and sometimes still is!—the favoured specific. Precious stones were often resorted to, if the traveller was fortunate enough to possess any, though some caution was required to make sure that it was the right sort. Jewels were associated with the birth month, and unless one had the right stone for the sign of the zodiac under which one was born one might well be more misfortunate than fortunate on the journey. It was, for instance, all right for those born under Aquarius or Libra to wear opals, but it was believed to be definitely unlucky for anyone else to do so (see page 54). This superstition can be met with to this day.

THE RABBIT'S PAW

BUT not everybody could afford to possess a jewel, not even one of the semi-precious stones, and for them (the great majority of a nation), safeguards had to be found which were less expensive. A rabbit's paw was a useful charm to carry in one's pocket. It was unlikely that a witch could harm you if you had that upon your person. It was a safeguard, too, for the poacher, who fancied that he could not be caught by a gamekeeper as long as he did not forget to slip the prized foot into one of his pockets before he set off on his night's prowl. Gamekeepers, on the other hand, felt safer from injury by violence if they carried a rabbit's foot upon them when they were trying to waylay the illegal abstracter of game from their employers' preserves.

WEARING COLOURS

SUPERSTITIOUS people often have their favourite colours, and believe that to wear garments of the particular ones they favour will bring them good luck and protect them from harm. In the past red was thought to be especially powerful to ward off danger. This is almost certainly why so much red is worn at ceremonial functions, why red carpets are laid down for important persons to walk upon, and why the colour figures so prominently in most national festivities. Blue, of course, has its votaries. It is a favourable colour for women to wear when going out of doors, especially the blue-eyed woman. And everybody knows that a bride should wear 'something blue' on her wedding-day, in order that Our Lady, whose favourite colour was supposed to be blue, might afford her her protection.

CARRYING LEAVES OF PLANTS

THE leaves of some plants were thought to be of some use in protecting from danger. Rosemary, clover, myrtle, pimpernel, laurel, were all once carried about by those who feared witches, and bunches of these and other herbs, together with sweet-scented flowers, were considered to ward off infection in time of plague or other epidemics. It is not so very long ago since it was customary to present a Judge with such a nosegay when he came to preside at a court of justice, the inference being that the prisoners brought before him might, after weeks of confinement in insanitary gaols, have contracted gaol fever with which they might infect him.

ST CHRISTOPHER MEDALS

A CUSTOM which is quite often in use today, is for the traveller to wear round the neck a medal depicting the image of St Christopher, the patron saint of travellers. It is not confined, as one might have supposed, to religious persons. People who subscribe to no religious denomination at all have been known to wear these medals. It would be interesting to know if those who have trusted to him for protection on their journeys will give up wearing the medals, now that doubt has arisen as to whether St Christopher ever existed. If he never had any existence, he could hardly be of use in affording protection to anybody.

SOME ANCIENT REMEDIES

An old folk-lore saying runs:

> For every evil under the sun
>   There is a remedy, or there is none!
> If there be one, try to find it,
>   If there be none, never mind it!

Whether or not our ancestors obeyed the second part of this injunction, they certainly seem to have done their utmost to comply with the first. Folk-lore is full of strange and often horrible remedies for every kind of ailment and disease, and the old alchemists and herbalists (the physicians of their day) spent most of their lives in searching for cures for them. The chief object of the alchemist's search, the philosophers' stone, was never found. Had the truly awful compounds those early chemists mixed and ground and boiled ever resulted in producing it, we should apparently never have needed to suffer any more from the ills that flesh 'is heir to', for it would have cured them all, as well as turning base metals into pure gold—the main reason for the quest. But they produced many weird recipes during their experiments, and there was hardly a plant in the whole of the known world which did not figure in their pharmacology, as we can see from the herbals of Gerard and

Culpeper. Reading some of their recipes, one wonders if many of the unexplained deaths of the Middle Ages were not due to their efforts to cure.

ABRACADABRA

ONE of the more harmless remedies resorted to by our forefathers was known as the Abracadabra, a magic word of oriental origin, sometimes said to have come from the ancient Egyptians, sometimes from the Hebrews. This was a charm widely-used in earlier ages. The word had to be written upon parchment, its letters set out in a particular way. Thus:

```
ABRACADABRA
 ABRACADABR
  ABRACADAB
   ABRACADA
    ABRACAD
     ABRACA
      ABRAC
       ABRA
        ABR
         AB
          A
```

The parchment was then suspended by a thread round the neck, when it was believed to be an infallible cure for ague, toothache, cramp, and almost any other sickness one can think of. It had to be written out by the physician, accompanied by a muttered incantation, the words of which could not be distinguished by the patient otherwise the magic would not work. If all had been done correctly and yet no cure resulted, the charm was not to be blamed. It was lack of sufficient faith on the part of the sufferer that inhibited the power of the spell.

Sometimes the mystic word was written out with the first letter omitted instead of the last. But it always had to be in the dagger shape when finished, with the letter A at the point.

INCANTATION CHARMS

INCANTATION charms were widely used in Britain at one time. These charms were comparatively harmless, except that they probably prevented the patient and his friends from consulting those who might have had greater knowledge to help. One such for a burn or a scald was frequently used in the last century:

> Out fire, in frost!
> In the name of the Father, Son, and
> Holy Ghost.

This had to be repeated nine times, with the healer making the sign of the cross, as he said the words over the affected part.

Another popular incantation was used to prevent a thorn from festering should one inadvertently be run into the flesh. The charm ran thus:

> Our Lord was the first man
> That ever thorn pricked upon:
> It never blistered, nor it never belted,
> And I pray God nor this not may.

CURES FOR WHOOPING-COUGH

THE incantation charms probably did little harm, but some of the others in vogue, even as late as the beginning of the present century, were a different matter. How many small children, suffering from whooping-cough, may not have succumbed to the 'cures' practised upon them? In some parts of Britain children with this disease were taken out of doors when the moon was new, their clothes removed and their chests and stomachs massaged for several minutes while the operator, gazing at the moon, repeated, for the usual nine times:

> What I see, may it increase,
> This disease, may it decrease;
> In the name of the Father, Son, and Holy Ghost, Amen.

Another remedy which must have been very bad for the child, as well as making him very frightened, was to dig a hole in a meadow and to place him in the hole head downwards. The turf was then placed over the child and he was left in this position until a cough was heard. It was thought that if the spell was carried out in the evening with only the parents there to witness it, the cough would soon be cured. Some healers recommended that the patient should be made to eat a roasted mouse, or to drink a broth made from an owl, while others said that a fox should be caught, that the child should carry a bowl of milk to it, and when the animal had drunk all it would of the milk, the patient should drink the rest.

In some places, which particular remedy should be tried was left to the judgment of a rider upon a piebald horse. The parents and friends of the little sufferer kept an anxious look-out for such a rider, and when one was seen, they would stop him and ask for his advice. Whatever he suggested would be tried. One hopes that he may often have advised calling in a doctor, and not any of the alarming nostrums in favour among the peasantry.

MANY of the bygone remedies of the British people were of a decidedly gruesome nature. The hand of a hanged man was thought to be very effective in many diseases. Wens, those troublesome and disfiguring cysts which, though harmless at first, may turn malignant in later life, were often rubbed by such a dead hand after an execution. Swellings of various kinds, varicose veins, and tuberculous glands, were considered to be much relieved by this treatment, and the crowds that gathered round the gallows when hangings took place in public did not only come to witness an exciting spectacle. Many of those who composed them came in hope of receiving some benefit for their complaints.

'A hair of the dog that bit you', which is still a well-known and oft-quoted proverb and used now to describe in a jocular manner the principle of homoeopathic medicine, was once a literal description of a cure for the bite of a mad dog. The dog having been killed, some of its hairs were cut off and the bitten person was instructed to eat them. At the same time a quantity of the hairs, fried or boiled were placed upon the bites together with some herb, rosemary was usually chosen, and the wounds bound up with clean rags. To finish off the treatment, the sign of the cross was then made over the bandage.

Mad dogs must have been very common in Britain during the sixteenth and seventeen centuries, to judge by the number of medicines for the cure of their bites contained in the Herbals of Gerard and Culpeper, and the treatises of many other medical writers of the time.

RHEUMATISM, CRAMP, AND GOUT

RHEUMATISM, cramp, and gout, loomed large among the afflictions of our forebears, if one may judge from the numerous recipes for their relief of which one reads. Many of them are still in use among country people. A potato carried in the pocket is often believed to allay the pains of rheumatism, and so does the wearing of a metal bracelet (copper for preference). One hears of instances of this last belief among educated persons, who talk vaguely of the combination of metal and flesh having something to do with electricity. Believers in the potato attempt no scientific explanation. They are content with the fact that their grandparents and great-grandparents swore by it, or that someone of their acquaintance had derived benefit from the practice, a practice which cannot be of very great antiquity in this country, since the potato was only introduced here in the sixteenth century, and even then was not in wide use, certainly not by the poor, for some two hundred years after its introduction. Taking the root of a mandrake to bed with one was a sovereign remedy for rheumatism in the Middle Ages, but only the better-off people could afford to do this since the mandrake was not indigenous in Britain and its price was high. The poor had to make do with the roots of briony, a plant which has always been plentiful in our hedgerows and which when fully-grown has a large root, not altogether dissimilar, apparently, to that of the mandrake.

The favourite remedy for cramp, that painful affliction which still troubles us though we no longer put it down to witchcraft as our ancestors did, was of much older origin. According to legend the remedy dates back to the time of

King Edward the Confessor. He received a magic ring, brought to him by pilgrims from Palestine, which gave him the power to heal by touching, a power which our monarchs were credited with possessing down to the days of Charles the Second. It seems to have vanished with the arrival of the House of Hanover. The Monarch's Touch was thought to be especially effective in cases of cramp and the 'Falling Sickness' of epilepsy, and crowds gathered whenever the king appeared in public, hoping to be touched and cured by the royal hand. Not everybody, of course, could get near enough to be touched by the ring, and somebody conceived the idea that the king should bless a number of rings which could be distributed to the sufferers, and which, it was supposed, would have the same effect as the monarch's touch. A formal ceremony of blessing took place on Good Friday in every year, when a basin of rings, usually made of some inferior metal, was presented to the sovereign during a religious service. These Cramp Rings, as they came to be called, were greatly prized by the recipients, for it was thought that the wearing of them would prevent the agonising attacks of this complaint.

The belief that cramp was due to the malevolence of some sorcerer was held in Britain for many centuries. It was certainly still prevalent in Shakespeare's day, and whether or not he believed in the superstition himself, few people in the audience would have thought it ridiculous that the dramatist should have made Prospero, the super-magician of *The Tempest*, subdue Caliban with the threat:

> If thou neglect'st, or dost unwillingly
> What I command, I'll rack thee with old cramps;
> Fill all thy bones with aches; make thee roar,
> That beasts shall tremble at thy din,

or be surprised that Caliban's rebellion should be instantly quelled.

Pieces of cork used often to be placed in the bed to prevent an attack of cramp during the night, and one can still find occasionally an old country man or woman wearing a cork garter. This is made from thin slivers of cork strung upon a ribbon or a piece of elastic, and worn around the knee. This is supposed to be very effective in warding off an attack of cramp. In some parts of England it is thought to be a good idea, since cramp so often attacks during the night, to place a pair of slippers under the bed with the soles upwards. Exactly how this was supposed to work never seems to have been explained, but those who practised the rite considered it to be infallible in preventing the painful spasm.

There are not very many folk-remedies for gout, which is mostly a complaint of the wealthier classes, but the old herbalists compounded medicines which they asserted would cure the trouble and probably found them profitable when administered to their richer patients. One of our wild plants was so often used in their nostrums that it acquired the name of goutwort, or goutweed which it bears to this day. Nicholas Culpeper says of it:

> Neither is it to be supposed that Goutweed hath its name for nothing; but upon experiment to heal the gout and sciatica; as also joint-aches and other cold griefs. The very bearing of it about one easeth the pain of the gout, and defends him that bears it from the disease.

WARTS

WARTS are rather mysterious growths. They have a habit of coming and going quite suddenly, which is possibly why superstition has credited so many people and so many remedies with having the power to cure them. Old men and women who practised White Magic specialised in the cure of warts. Sometimes they rubbed them with herbs, muttering incantations the while. Sometimes the incantations alone were thought to be effective. If no White Witch was available, there were still plenty of things to be done by the sufferer. The patient could stand in the light of the full moon and rub the wart; or if he could gain access to a dead person he could stroke the growth with a dead hand. A very favourite remedy, and one that has been in use during the present century, was to obtain a piece of raw beef—preferably to steal it, the cure was more certain if the meat was stolen—tie it firmly over the wart and leave it on overnight. In the morning the meat was to be buried in the ground, as it decayed the wart would waste away.

Rubbing with something that was afterwards buried or shut up in a box to rot was a very popular treatment for a wart, or, indeed, for any kind of swelling. It sometimes involved much cruelty, as when a live toad, mouse, spider, or other small creature was used for the experiment. However, sometimes the method was harmless enough as when a bean pod was used for the rubbing and afterwards buried under an ash tree, the patient repeating the couplet:

> As this bean shall rot away,
> So my wart shall soon decay.

To ensure success, the operation had to be done secretly and at night. A similar operation was done with a stick of green elder, the words of the rhyme being altered slightly to make them appropriate.

Another harmless expedient was to take a piece of string and to tie in it as many knots as there were warts to be cured. Then, having touched each wart with a knot, a different knot for each wart, the operator was instructed to throw the string over the shoulder into some place where it would soon decay—a pond, or a hole in the ground previously prepared was recommended. In due course the warts would disappear.

HOLY WELLS

MANY wells and fountains were held in superstitious reverence in the past for the supposed healing quality of their waters. Some, of course, did have certain medicinal virtues; those that contained iron, for instance, or traces of sulphur. A prolonged course of drinking such waters would no doubt have proved of benefit to the sick—the treatment is still prescribed occasionally today. But bygone ages believed almost every well to hold a magical power of healing and death must have been hastened for many people by their friends carrying them from their sick beds to be bathed in the holy water of some famed healing well. Even as late as the last century it was quite customary to see the trees and bushes surrounding some country spring decorated with bits of rag, or sometimes with whole garments, left there by devotees to propitiate the guardian spirit of the water. These scraps of clothing were a debased form of the really valuable gifts that were brought by the Romans in ancient times in return for favours of healing received, or in the hope of receiving. What good such relics would be to the spirit was never explained, though the coins which were sometimes thrown into the water in gratitude might have been acceptable to the mortal guardians of the well if not to the spiritual ones.

WEDDING-RINGS AS HEALERS

THE rather painful and disfiguring boil that sometimes occurs on the eyelid, known as a stye, is still occasionally treated by rubbing with a wedding-ring. It must, however, be a *gold* ring, the fashionable platinum wedding-ring, or a ring made of any metal other than gold is said to be quite useless by the advocates of this treatment. And it should be a ring worn by a happy and virtuous wife, otherwise the healing power will probably be too feeble to effect a cure.

A wedding-ring is also supposed to be efficacious in helping a cut to heal if it is gently rubbed along the wound. A variation of this belief is that the cut should be stroked by the finger wearing the ring. If the finger is clean, this might be a more hygienic treatment.

WHITE HEATHER

THERE are a diversity of opinions about white heather, which is occasionally found growing among the more ordinary purple-flowered plants. Some count it as a lucky flower and wear it to bring them good fortune. But there are others who say it is definitely an ill luck bringer, and cite in support a tradition that a sprig of it was given to Bonnie Prince Charlie when he landed in Scotland in August 1745. Everyone knows how that ill-fated expedition turned out. Both schools of thought, though, might agree about the flower's healing power—it is supposed that the wearing of it will cure the drunkard's craving for drink. This idea probably arose because at one time the brewing of heather beer was a thriving trade in places where the plant grew in abundance. The appearance of a plant bearing white flowers instead of the usual purple ones perhaps suggested to our imaginative countrymen that the genius of the plant disapproved of beer drinking and might infect its wearer with the same distaste. No cure, however, seems ever to have been reported.

* * *

THIS book contains only some of the better-known superstitions which in the past—and occasionally still today—have plagued the minds of men. Doubtless every reader will know of a few that have been left out, for they are innumerable, and are, in fact, being created every day by imaginative people. Let anything unusual occur, either good or bad, and the superstitious will cast back to see what might have caused it. Had they departed from their usual custom in some way, worn something different, seen something new? Yes, of course, they had! It must have been such-and-such a thing they did or said or saw that brought about the phenomenon—and another superstitious belief is added to their already vast store.

Let Shakespeare have the last words upon this subject, words which he put into the mouth of Cardinal Pandulph in his play of *King John*:

> No natural exhalation in the sky,
>   No scape of nature, no distemper'd day,
> No common wind, no customed event,
>   But they will pluck away his natural cause
> And call them meteors, prodigies, and signs,
>   Abortives, presages, and tongues of heaven,
>   Plainly denouncing vengeance—

BIBLIOGRAPHY

JOHN BRAND   *Popular Antiquities of Great Britain*

SIR J. G. FRASER   *The Golden Bough*
Folk Lore in The Old Testament

CHRISTINA HOLE   *Witchcraft in England*

T. F. THISELTON DYER   *British Popular Customs*
English Folk Lore

NICHOLAS CULPEPER   *Complete Herbal*

JOHN GERARD   *Herball*

JAMES ORCHARD HALLIWELL   *Nursery Rhymes of England*

PHILIPP SCHMIDT S.J.   *Superstition and Magic*

E. & M. A. RADFORD   *Encyclopaedia of Superstitions* (Edited by Christina Hole)

JOHN L. RAYNER   *Proverbs and Maxims*

M. OLDFIELD HOWEY   *The Horse In Magic And Myth*

WILLIAM JONES F.S.A.   *Credulities Past and Present*

ANNE PRATT   *The Flowering Plants, Grasses, Sedges and Ferns of Great Britain*

SIR PAUL HARVEY   *The Oxford Companion to English Literature*

THE REV. DR BREWER   *Dictionary of Phrase And Fable*

SIR WILLIAM SMITH   *Everyman's Smaller Classical Dictionary*
JOHN GAY   *The Fables*

INDEX